ESTELLE TJIPUKA
BEST SELLING AUTHOR OF ***BREAKING BARRIERS***

BREAKING
—— INTO THE ——
BOARDROOM
A GUIDE FOR WOMEN

First published by Estelle Tjipuka
© 2025 Estelle Tjipuka

ISBN: 9781049206677 (print)

Cover and Interior crafted with love by the team at:
www.myebook.online

All rights reserved. No part of this book may be reproduced, stored in a retrievable system or transmitted in any form by any means, electronic, mechanical, photocopying, recording or otherwise, without the written permission of the copyright owner, with the exception of verbal quotes and referencing directly from the book.

Dear _____

You were never meant to play small.

You are a leader – not someday, not when you feel "ready", but right now. The boardroom needs your voice, your insight, your intuition, and your lived experience. Your presence is not a privilege – it's a powerful necessity.

There will be moments when the doors seem locked, when your confidence wavers, or when you wonder if you're too much or not enough. But I want you to remember this: **you are already everything you need to be.** Growth will refine you, but greatness is already within you.

Let this book be your mirror, your compass, and your permission slip to rise.

Stand tall. Speak up. Take your seat.

And when there is no seat – build your own table.

Your story is still unfolding, and the best chapters are yet to come.

With fierce belief in your brilliance,

Estelle

To my beloved daughters, **Keasha and Kayla Tjipuka**,
You are my greatest inspiration. May you always walk boldly in your purpose, never doubting your worth or your immense potential. The world is waiting for your brilliance – lead with confidence, integrity, and courage. Break barriers, redefine possibilities, and never settle for anything less than what you deserve. I believe in you, always.

To the **ten extraordinary women in Namibia's financial sector** *who generously shared their experiences, insights, and wisdom, Your voices are powerful, and your journeys are a testament to the resilience and excellence of women in leadership. Thank you for contributing to this book and, more importantly, for paving the way for others to follow. Your impact reaches far beyond boardrooms – it is shaping the future of leadership for generations to come.*

To my husband, **Erwin Tjipuka**,
Your unwavering support, encouragement, and belief in me have been my anchor throughout this journey. Thank you for standing by my side, for being my sounding board, and for championing my dreams as fiercely as your own. I am deeply grateful.

This book is a tribute to all of you. May it serve as a beacon of empowerment for women everywhere, inspiring them to take their rightful place at the table.

CONTENTS

Introduction	vii
1. Rise and Lead	1
2. Identifying the Dream Blockers	14
3. The Foundation of Leadership Success	29
4. Building Unshakeable Confidence	45
5. Coaching and Mentorship	62
6. Visualise Your Goal	76
7. Position Yourself for Promotion	93
8. Addressing Work–Life Imbalances	110
9. Balancing Ambition, Wellness, and Home	124
10. The Power of Personal Branding	144
About the Author	163

INTRODUCTION

The boardroom is more than just a meeting space – it is the epicentre of power and authority, where decisions shape industries, economies, and societies. Those who occupy these seats do not merely run companies; they influence the lives of billions, dictate market trends, and drive national economic policies. Given the boardroom's immense significance, it is imperative to ensure equal representation of both men and women at the table.

As women, we possess the intelligence, strategic insight, and resilience necessary to drive organisational success. We are bold, intuitive, and tenacious, continuously pushing boundaries and unlocking potential – both our own and that of our organisations. While we lead with vision and innovation, we also bring a transformative and nurturing approach to leadership. Above all, we are driven by a deep commitment to making a lasting impact on the world.

Yet, for far too long, women's presence in boardrooms has been limited. Our voices have been muted, and our leadership potential underestimated. We continue to face biases and stereotypes that challenge our rise. While affirmative action policies have enabled progress, much work remains. It is up to us to overcome these obstacles – not just to break into the boardroom but to thrive within it.

This book is a call to action. A roadmap. A coaching tool. It is written for every woman who dares to dream beyond societal constraints. Whether you are a corporate executive, an entrepreneur striving to scale your business, or a rising leader navigating workplace politics, *Breaking into the Boardroom* will equip you with the strategies, mindset, and resilience needed to claim your seat at the table – and own it with confidence.

WHY THE BOARDROOM MATTERS – FOR EVERY WOMAN

Breaking into the boardroom is about more than corporate leadership; it is about influence, economic empowerment, and legacy-building. Whether you are at the helm of a multinational corporation, a government institution, or your own business, the principles of governance, strategy, and leadership remain essential.

For entrepreneurs, the boardroom represents even greater opportunities. It signifies financial independence, business longevity, and access to capital and partnerships that drive growth. A woman who understands boardroom dynamics is not just a business owner; she is a leader capable of scaling her company, securing investment, and shaping industry standards.

Too often, women-led businesses remain small scale because their owners focus on daily operations rather than governance and long-term sustainability. This book aims to shift that

INTRODUCTION

mindset. It is time for women entrepreneurs to see themselves not only as business owners but as industry leaders.

THE JOURNEY TO LEADERSHIP: MY STORY

My boardroom journey began in 2006 when I was appointed as a Non-Executive Director on the Board of the Development Bank of Namibia (DBN). Being in my early thirties, this appointment was a moment of immense pride and validation. It affirmed that I belonged at the table and could contribute meaningfully at the highest levels of decision-making.

That was just the beginning.

Between 2006 and 2008, I spearheaded the establishment of Namibia's first-ever Financial Intelligence Centre (FIC) – a landmark initiative that positioned me at the forefront of our national strategy to combat financial crime. This pioneering role gave me access to the Bank of Namibia's Management Committee (MC), where I gained valuable insight into high-level deliberations and strategic decisions. I was subsequently appointed Deputy Director of Financial Investigations and Analysis, while also serving as Acting Director of the FIC.

In November 2009, I was appointed Director of Finance and Administration at the Bank of Namibia – a role that reaffirmed my seat on the Management Committee and expanded my executive responsibilities within the institution.

In 2010, I became a Non-Executive Director of the Namibia Financial Supervisory Authority (NAMFISA) – Namibia's regulator for the Non-Bank Financial Institutions and by 2013, I had the honour of serving as its chairperson. During the same period, I also served as a Director on NAMFISA's Appeal Board.

INTRODUCTION

The journey was not without its challenges. Women in leadership were still rare, and boardrooms remained predominantly male and often unwelcoming. My age, race, and gender were scrutinised. I encountered resistance in the form of stereotyping, corporate bullying, and subtle exclusion. Each time, I faced a choice: allow these barriers to hold me back or rise above them. I chose to rise, fuelling my passion to bring more women into leadership roles.

With over 28 years of corporate and professional experience, I have served on more than six boards across Namibia's public and private sectors. At the time of writing this book, I chair the Board of Directors for the Namibian Diamond Trading Company (NDTC) and serve as a Board Member of Sanlam Namibia Holdings. In 2019, I was privileged to serve on the Presidential High-Level Panel on the Namibian Economy (HLPNE), appointed by the late President His Excellency Dr Hage G. Geingob. Additionally, I served on the Short-term Insurance Advisory Committee.

Over the years, I have mentored countless women. As an Executive, Business, and Transformational Coach, Speaker, and Author, I empower my clients – many of whom are women – to build confidence, sharpen their skills, and expand their networks to break barriers and step into leadership. Through this book, I aim to do the same for you.

WHO IS THIS BOOK FOR?

This book will guide every ambitious woman seeking to elevate her leadership journey. Whether you are:

- entering corporate, politics, or an NGO,
- a mid-level manager aspiring to senior leadership,

- a senior executive looking to strengthen your influence,
- or a business owner aiming to scale your impact.

Leadership is not just a possibility for you – it is a calling you are fully capable of embracing. You will learn from women who, like you, defied the odds and shattered the corporate glass ceiling. Together, we will dismantle negative thought patterns, cultivate confidence and resilience, and map out a strategic path to success. From positioning yourself for promotions to leveraging mentorship and sponsorship, this book will equip you with the tools to claim your rightful seat at the table.

STRATEGY, RESILIENCE, AND THE ROAD AHEAD

The renowned Chinese military strategist Sun Tzu says in *The Art of War*:

"If you know the enemy and know yourself, you need not fear the result of a hundred battles."

His wisdom underscores the power of self-awareness and strategy in overcoming obstacles. To break into the boardroom, you must:

- **Know Yourself** – Understand your strengths, values, and leadership potential.
- **Know the Barriers** – Recognise biases, systemic challenges, and the corporate glass ceiling.
- **Execute Strategically** – Leverage your skills, challenge limitations, and position yourself for success.

INTRODUCTION

By mastering both your internal strengths and external challenges, you will eliminate fear and take control of your leadership journey.

In this book, we will explore the complexities of the corporate glass ceiling – how it functions and, most importantly, how you can break through it. Leadership is not just about reaching the top; it is about sustaining success and making a lasting impact.

THE FUTURE IS FEMALE – AND IT BEGINS NOW

While I was writing this book, Namibia made history by democratically electing its first female President, Her Excellency Dr Netumbo Nandi-Ndaitwah – a defining moment in our nation's political and leadership journey. A seasoned diplomat, freedom fighter, and visionary leader, she embodies the strength, resilience, and excellence of Namibian women. Her ascent to the highest office is not only a personal triumph but a powerful symbol for every girl and woman who dares to dream beyond limitations. It affirms that leadership has no gender – and the time for women to lead boldly and unapologetically is now.

Yet, progress remains uneven. Many talented, capable women hesitate, held back by self-doubt and systemic biases. That stops today.

This book is not just about breaking barriers – it's about building legacies. It's about ensuring that the next generation of women will not have to fight as hard for their seat at the table because we have paved the way.

The boardroom awaits. Your leadership journey begins now.

INTRODUCTION

**Welcome to
Breaking into the Boardroom
- A Guide for Women -**

Let's get started.

CHAPTER 1
RISE AND LEAD

"Great leaders prioritise the interests of others before their own."

American football coach Vince Lombardi once said, "Leaders aren't born, they are made. And they are made just like anything else, through hard work." This quote speaks to a fundamental question many of us have asked ourselves on our journey to leadership: "Do I have the leadership gene inside me?" Whether you have led successfully before or are facing new leadership challenges, this question arises. We often believe certain people are destined to lead while others are not. We assume that fate has endowed some with leadership qualities while skipping over the rest of us. We perceive these individuals as natural-born leaders – those who were simply born with it.

Like Lombardi, I do not subscribe to the notion that only a select few are meant to lead. There are no natural-born followers – we all possess leadership potential. The difference lies in our willingness to develop and refine that potential. Manifesting leadership and breaking into the boardroom requires hard work, resilience, and determination. It demands that we go through the fire and emerge stronger, much like gold being refined to remove impurities. Gold endures temperatures exceeding a thousand degrees Celsius, but becomes more valuable and durable afterwards.

Every leader you see in the boardroom has faced and overcome career and personal challenges. Leadership is not handed out on a silver platter; it is fought for and earned. Work and life challenges will always test your resolve, making you question whether you have what it takes to be the leader you hoped to be. With every challenge, you must respond with an emphatic YES! This resilience and determination are essential tools to help you break into the boardroom and stay there.

EMBRACING THE LEADERSHIP JOURNEY

As women aspiring to lead, we must remember that the path to leadership is forged through perseverance and a willingness to overcome obstacles. Challenges are not meant to be avoided but embraced, confronted head-on, and conquered. These challenges are stepping stones to success in the boardroom. The saying "Heavy is the head that wears the crown" is no understatement – leadership is about responsibility. Everything rises and falls on leadership. As a leader, the buck stops with you. When challenges arise, you cannot pass the responsibility onto someone else. Instead, overcoming them builds your capacity to handle even greater responsibilities.

The good news? You do not have to face these challenges alone. I am here to guide you through your leadership journey. The fact that you are reading this book tells me that you are already on the path to leadership. Your willingness to invest in your personal development demonstrates your belief in yourself and your potential.

THE POWER OF SERVANT LEADERSHIP

Clarity precedes execution. If you still have reservations about whether you have what it takes to lead at a high level, know that this uncertainty is normal. Often, it stems from a lack of clarity on what leadership truly means. In my view, leadership is best defined as serving others. It is about creating an environment where others can thrive.

Great leaders prioritise the interests of others before their own. Genuine investment in the advancement of others is what propels individuals into positions of power – and keeps them there. This might seem counterintuitive in a world where many believe that climbing the corporate ladder requires ruthless competition and relentless self-promotion. However, in my experience, decision makers look for leaders who prioritise organisational success over personal ambition.

Promotions are never granted in a vacuum of self-interest. Instead, they go to those who have demonstrated a commitment to the betterment of their colleagues and the organisation. Understanding this principle is crucial for women aspiring to lead. By focusing on serving others and fostering an environment where everyone can succeed, you pave the way for your advancement and establish a foundation for impactful leadership.

LESSONS FROM TRAILBLAZING NAMIBIAN WOMEN

True leadership in corporate settings is about serving your clients, colleagues, and company. This is the key to the boardroom. Women have a natural advantage in leadership because serving others is ingrained in who we are. Across all aspects of life, women give selflessly to benefit their families, friends, and communities. A servant's heart is the compass that will guide you to success in both your personal and professional life.

Consider the journey of Ms Nangula Uaandja. In 2000, she made history as the first Black woman in Namibia to qualify as a Chartered Accountant. Her achievement was more than a personal milestone – it became a beacon of inspiration for countless women, including myself, determined to break barriers in corporate Namibia and beyond.

A true trailblazer, Ms Uaandja later went on to become the first Black Namibian to serve as CEO of Pricewaterhouse-Coopers Namibia, and later held the esteemed role of President of the Institute of Chartered Accountants of Namibia. In 2021, she was appointed CEO of the Namibia Investment Promotion and Development Board by the late President H.E. Dr Hage G. Geingob.

Her journey into accounting began not with ambition for accolades, but with a personal mission: to help her father resolve a tax liability that threatened their family business. Initially drawn to a career in science, she pivoted to commerce, and eventually discovered her true calling in accounting – a decision that would lay the foundation for a career defined by excellence and impact. After receiving the 2011 Namibia Businesswoman of the Year award, Ms Uaandja deepened her focus on leadership and economic development. She used her unique access to leaders across the public and private sectors to explore the root causes of Namibia's pressing social challenges – unemployment, poverty, and inequality. This journey ignited a deeper goal within her; not just to lead but to be part of the solution.

Motivated by this purpose, she pursued a Master's and Doctorate in Business Leadership. Eventually, she made the bold decision to leave behind a 24-year career in the private sector to serve the public. Her transition was not just a career move – it was a call to serve her country with intention and integrity.

Ms Uaandja's story is a powerful testament to servant leadership. Her unwavering commitment to her family, her community, and her nation has shaped a legacy that transcends titles and positions. She reminds us that leadership is not about power or prestige, but about purpose, service, and impact.

By embracing a servant's heart, you too can chart your path to leadership – breaking barriers, lifting others, and leaving a legacy that matters.

Similarly, Ms Leonie Dunn, my former boss, became the first Director of the Financial Intelligence Centre of the Republic of Namibia, and subsequently the first female Deputy Governor of the Bank of Namibia. A lawyer by profession and an extraordinary leader, she embodies a powerful leadership motto: "In life, serve with passion, dedication, respect, and without fear or favour. Always give your very best, no matter how small the task. Do all the good you can, for as long as you can, for whomever you can." Ms Dunn's motto embodies servant leadership, integrity, and excellence. True leaders serve with passion and dedication, treating others with respect while making ethical decisions without fear or favour. Leadership is about giving your best in every task, no matter how small, and making a lasting impact by doing good for as long as possible, for as many as possible.

Selfish individuals rarely become effective leaders. If they do, their tenures are usually short-lived due to a lack of influence. Influence is the foundation of leadership. If you cannot inspire others to follow your direction, you cannot lead. Benjamin Franklin aptly stated, "A man wrapped up in himself makes a very small bundle." In modern terms, a self-centred life limits your impact. Leadership is about creating value for as many people as possible, thereby expanding your influence. The more people you positively impact, the greater your influence will be. For women aspiring to lead, understanding this principle is crucial. Your ability to serve and uplift others will ultimately determine your success and effectiveness as a leader.

Ms Baronice Hans is a trailblazer in Banking and Finance, who became the second Black woman in Namibia to qualify as a Chartered Accountant and the first woman to be appointed as Managing Director of a commercial bank in Namibia. She also made history as the first woman to chair the Bankers Association of Namibia. Her leadership has shattered barriers for women in the financial sector, paving the way for future generations. Since her appointment, more women have risen to high positions within the banking industry.

Former Prime Minister Saara Kuugongelwa-Amadhila is a true trailblazer, shattering barriers in Namibia. At just 27, she joined the cabinet boardroom as Director General of the National Planning Commission, paving the way for future female leaders. Her visionary leadership led to her historic appointment as Namibia's first female Finance Minister in 2003. In 2015, she made history again as Namibia's first female Prime Minister, further cementing her legacy as a pioneer and servant leader. At the time of writing, she had taken yet another groundbreaking step as the first female Speaker of the National Assembly, continuing to shape Namibia's political landscape.

You can only influence people who believe you genuinely care about them. Theodore Roosevelt wisely said, "People do not care how much you know until they know how much you care." To lead effectively, you must earn trust by demonstrating a genuine commitment to the aspirations and wellbeing of those you lead. When people see that you have their best interests at heart, they will follow you with confidence and loyalty.

- *Understanding What Matters*

The first step in showing you care is understanding what drives your clients, colleagues, and organisation. What are their goals? What motivates them? Clients seek timely, professional solutions and want to feel valued for choosing your services. Colleagues aim to achieve their Key Performance Indicators (KPIs), advance in their careers, and support their families. Companies focus on growth, industry leadership, and profitability for stakeholders.

- *Taking Action*

The second step is to actively contribute to the success of these key stakeholders. Leadership is about adding value and solving problems. To step into your full leadership potential, become a "solution centre" for those you lead. Bring insights, support, and tangible results to the table while consistently demonstrating your commitment to their growth and success.

By understanding and acting on these principles, you will build the trust and influence necessary to lead effectively and inspire those around you.

LEADING IN A MULTIGENERATIONAL WORKPLACE

At this point, you might be thinking, "Estelle, surely showing people you care and serving them isn't the only way to influence them. I've seen leaders – some even authoritarian – give orders, and people follow without question." You're right. Leadership comes in different styles, and what you're describing is autocratic leadership. While this approach may have yielded results in the past, it is no longer effective in today's workplace.

The modern workforce is multigenerational, with each generation bringing unique perspectives, values, and expectations. As a leader, you can no longer rely on a one-size-fits-all approach. You must adapt to lead a workforce that may span five distinct generations, each with different views on leadership, work ethic, and motivation. Simply barking orders and expecting compliance won't cut it.

UNDERSTANDING GENERATIONAL DIFFERENCES

Over the past decade, extensive research has gone into understanding what motivates different generations. This knowledge is crucial for leaders seeking to build high-performing teams. While there is some debate on exact birth years, the generally accepted generational breakdown is as follows:

- Baby Boomers (1946 – 1964) → Aged 61–79 in 2025
- Generation X (1965 –1980) → Aged 45–60 in 2025
- Millennials (1981 – 1996) → Aged 29–44 in 2025
- Generation Z (1997 – 2012) → Aged 13–28 in 2025
- Generation A (2013 – Current) → Aged 12 in 2025

BABY BOOMERS: THE LEGACY LEADERS

Although Baby Boomers now make up the smallest segment of the workforce, they still hold many key leadership positions. Their seniority, resilience, and dedication make them the gatekeepers of promotions and leadership opportunities.

Boomers are known for their loyalty – many have spent their entire careers at one company and take pride in long-term service. They see work as life and are not strong advocates for work–life balance. Even in retirement, many continue contributing through consulting, mentoring, or volunteer roles.

Strategies to Lead Boomers:

- Show respect for their experience and contributions.
- Demonstrate commitment, hard work, and loyalty – these are values they admire.
- Tap into their wisdom and mentorship to strengthen intergenerational collaboration.

GENERATION X: THE INDEPENDENT ACHIEVERS

Generation X, raised in the aftermath of the Baby Boomers' intense work ethic, values work–life balance more than their predecessors. Often called "The Divorce Generation," they grew up witnessing high divorce rates, recessions, and corporate downsizing. As a result, they tend to be more independent, entrepreneurial, and sceptical of job loyalty as a path to security.

They want fair compensation, professional growth, and job satisfaction – and they won't hesitate to leave if they don't get it. Having grown up in dual-income or single-parent households, they are self-reliant and dislike micromanagement.

Strategies to Lead Gen X:

- Respect their independence and avoid micromanagement.
- Offer professional development opportunities to keep them engaged.
- Provide flexibility – they value their personal lives as much as their careers.

MILLENNIALS: THE PURPOSE DRIVEN WORKFORCE

Millennials are currently the largest generation in the workforce and will continue to dominate leadership pipelines in the coming years. They demand more than just a salary – they want purpose, growth, and inclusivity in the workplace.

This generation values collaboration, mentorship, and feedback. They seek flexible work arrangements, career advancement opportunities, and workplaces that align with their values – especially companies that support diversity, mental health, and social responsibility.

Strategies to Lead Millennials:

- Foster collaborative work environments – they thrive in teamwork.
- Provide regular feedback – they value coaching and mentorship.
- Support work–life balance and offer meaningful work that aligns with their values.

GENERATION Z: THE DIGITAL NATIVES

By 2030, Generation Z will make up 30% of the global workforce. Unlike Millennials, they are more independent, direct, and pragmatic. Having grown up in the digital era, they are tech-savvy, adaptable, and resourceful.

They prefer clear expectations, direct feedback, and opportunities for rapid growth. While Millennials value collaboration, Gen Z leans towards autonomy and self-sufficiency. They expect companies to prioritise mental health, diversity, and work–life integration.

Strategies to Lead Gen Z:

- Be transparent and direct – they appreciate clarity over sugarcoating.
- Offer freedom and flexibility – they value autonomy.
- Embrace technology – they expect digital efficiency in the workplace.

GENERATION ALPHA: THE FUTURE CHANGE-MAKERS

Born from 2013 onward, Generation Alpha will enter the workforce by 2035. Raised in a tech-saturated world, they are digital natives influenced by Artificial Intelligence, online learning, and global connectivity. They are expected to be highly creative, socially aware, and purpose driven.

Strategies to Lead Gen Alpha:

- Integrate technology and innovation into leadership and learning.
- Encourage creativity and interactive problem-solving.

- Foster emotional safety, inclusivity, and mental wellness.
- Embrace global thinking – they'll expect leaders to act with purpose and social responsibility.

Preparing to lead Gen Alpha means building agile, inclusive, and digitally empowered workplaces that align with their values and expectations.

LEADING A DIVERSE WORKFORCE: INSIGHTS FOR WOMEN

Deloitte's *2024 Gen Z and Millennial Survey* highlights that these two generations have redefined workplace expectations, demanding more from employers than ever before. They seek supportive leaders, meaningful work, and organisations that advocate for social causes. Additionally, they prioritise flexible work conditions, competitive compensation, mental health support, and opportunities for continuous growth and development.

While Millennials and Generation Z share some core values, they also have distinct expectations. Research shows that Millennials thrive in collaborative environments and prefer constructive feedback, while Gen Z individuals value autonomy and appreciate direct feedback. These differences, along with those of Baby Boomers and Generation X, underscore the need for adaptable leadership that meets the needs of a multigenerational workforce.

No matter your level of leadership, you must engage everyone. As a leader, it's your responsibility to draw the best out of each individual. Effective leadership is about making people want to work with you, leading by influence rather than manipulation, and setting an example rather than relying on a title. As demonstrated by the inspirational women we discussed earlier, breaking into the boardroom is rewarding but comes with great responsibility.

SUMMARY: RISE AND LEAD

This chapter affirms a timeless truth: leadership is not a birthright – it's a choice, shaped through hard work, resilience, and purpose. Every woman has the potential to lead, not by seeking titles, but by serving others with intention and integrity. Through the inspiring journeys of trailblazing Namibian women, we see that servant leadership opens doors to lasting impact.

In today's multigenerational and diverse workforce, effective leadership demands empathy, adaptability, and a deep understanding of what drives people. Influence, not authority, is the true currency of leadership. By choosing to serve, staying grounded in your values, and leading with courage, you too can rise – break into the boardroom, and lead with power, purpose, and heart.

Now that you understand what true leadership requires, it's time to chart your own path. But before we develop a winning strategy, we must first confront and dismantle the dream blockers – those internal and external barriers that have made you question your worth and your right to lead.

These blockers often cloud our vision, convincing us that leadership is reserved for others, not for us. But that's simply not true. You have a voice, a vision, and value to bring to the table.

In the next chapter, we'll uncover these hidden forces that hold many women back, so that you can rise above them confidently and clearly.

CHAPTER 2
IDENTIFYING THE DREAM BLOCKERS

"The barriers that we face as women are significant, but they are not insurmountable."

The night before his assassination on 4 April 1968, Martin Luther King Jr spoke with striking clarity about the future he believed in. He acknowledged the hardships ahead but spoke with peace and certainty – not because the road was easy, but because he had already seen the destination in his mind's eye. Before the vision of a free and equal America became reality, he had to go there in his heart. He had to climb above the chaos of the moment and picture a better world – the Promised Land, not yet visible, but deeply real to him.

This kind of vision isn't physical. It's not about what the eyes can see, but what the heart – the subconscious mind – can believe. The mountain he spoke of symbolised the difficulties he and his people faced due to segregation, and the uphill battle they faced. But his victory lay in his ability to see beyond those challenges. He chose to see possibility amid glaring impossibility.

VISUALISING YOURSELF IN THE BOARDROOM

Likewise, as a woman leader, breaking into the boardroom starts within. You first have to see yourself in the boardroom before you occupy it and take your seat. This is because you cannot achieve what you have not seen with your mind. At some point, the dream must evolve from a vague idea to a clear picture in your head. Before we go any further, I want you to take a moment and answer this question sincerely. Do you see yourself in the boardroom? If you do, what does it look like? Which one is your seat at the table? What are you wearing? What decisions are you making to take your company to the next level? Who are you inspiring and elevating? If you can see the answers to these questions with clarity, then you are on your way to the boardroom. If not, then there are some hindrances to your dream that we might need to address. I call these dream blockers.

OVERCOMING DREAM BLOCKERS

- *Silencing the Internal Noise*

Just as Martin Luther King Jr did, you are going to have to overcome your limitations to reach the mountaintop and see the promised land. I don't know about you, but when I think of a mountaintop I see a quiet and peaceful place with a clear 360-degree view of the land beneath it. There is clarity of vision and direction on the mountaintop, therefore, you need to silence the noise of your dream blockers for you to get there. It is only you who has the power to do this because the noise they make is internal. It can only be heard by you, so it is only you who can shut it down. Granted, most of these dream blockers might have emanated from external voices and circumstances, but it is you who ultimately gave them the voice within.

- *Paradigm Shifts: Rewiring the Mind for Success*

Not only that, but you might also have amplified these voices by believing them over a long time. This allowed them to reinforce their negative messages in your mind over and over again, creating pathways or tracks for limiting thoughts. These pathways or tracks became the paradigm or filter through which all your decisions were made. This means you might want to break into the boardroom, but the filter through which your thoughts run will ultimately cause you to think that you cannot achieve that dream.

You cannot live beyond your thought life. It does not matter how much you try. As much as this is a sobering truth, the good news is that you can create a new filter that empowers thoughts of victory and success. This is what is referred to as a paradigm shift. A change of the lens through which you see yourself and life in general. How you see yourself is the foundation for success in everything that you do. You have to see yourself as capable, adequate, and deserving if you are going to make it to the top. You also have to see life as fair and rewarding to those – like you – who are willing to put in the work. Life is good. It takes what you give it and multiplies it back to you. All you have to do is amplify the voices of dream-enabling and empowering thoughts.

- *Building a New Narrative*

After completing Chapter 1, I know you were stirred up to rise and become the leader you were born to be. You saw the amazing women who defied the odds to become iconic boardroom leaders, and you said to yourself, "If they can do it, I can do it too." That is a dream-enabling and empowering thought, and the moment you said that, you gave an inner voice to it. You sowed the seed for a new way of thinking. A new paradigm that you have to consciously build upon and strengthen. You have to be intentional about it. Why? Because the inner voices of dream blockers are not silenced at the flick of a switch. It does not happen overnight. You have to train your mind over a long time to consistently choose dream-enabling thoughts over dream blockers. As the voice of your dream-enabling thoughts becomes louder, it will eventually drown out the voice of the dream blockers.

THE INNER BATTLE: SELF-DOUBT

- *Identifying Self-Doubt*

The worst kind of dream blockers are those that seek to prevent you from even dreaming of breaking into the boardroom. They say to you, "How dare you even think you can achieve anything, let alone break into the boardroom? Who do you think you are? Your kind does not get promoted to that level. You are just average. Look at all these mistakes you have made in the past. If you failed then, you will certainly fail now. Just stop, you are going to embarrass yourself." As women, we hear these voices to varying degrees. These are voices of self-doubt, and their main goal is to kill our self-confidence.

- *What is Self-Confidence?*

My definition of self-confidence is trusting in one's judgement, abilities, and qualities. Self-doubt will try to convince you that you are lacking in these three key areas. Firstly, it will tell you that you are not a good decision-maker. You will never make the right decisions to get you into the boardroom, and if you get in there, by some stroke of luck, your poor decision-making will get you kicked out. Secondly, it will tell you that even if you make it into the boardroom, you will not be able to thrive there. Thirdly, it will convince you that you just do not have the attributes of an executive. Self-doubt will remind you of all your flaws and make you believe you'll never measure up. It will make you see executives as superhumans that you cannot match up to, a special breed of perfect people who do not make any mistakes or have any weaknesses.

- *Fighting the Lies of Self-Doubt*

I do not know about you, but I have had my fair share of encounters with self-doubt. Every time I had a new assignment on my table, it would raise its ugly head and try to convince me that I could not make it. In fighting and overcoming this sneaky enemy, I realised that not only was it a liar, but it was also an exaggerator. It is not true that you are not a good decision-maker. The success that you have achieved in life so far demonstrates that you have sound judgement. Reading this book on your quest to become more in life shows that you are capable of making great decisions.

Self-doubt seeks to put you in a "you will never" box, which is a creation of exaggeration. You might have made some errors in judgement in the past, but that does not define who you are. It does not mean you should carry the label of Bad Decision-

Maker for the rest of your life. Mistakes happen, but the beauty of life is that we can learn to get better at anything. There are tools and techniques that you can employ to become a better decision-maker. It is the same when it comes to your abilities. You can always learn and perfect new skills through training.

When it comes to qualities, it is important to know that no one is perfect. Executives are normal human beings just like you and me. They have their doubts and insecurities that they face, and they also make mistakes. What sets them apart is their ability to thrive regardless of their imperfections. They do not let their flaws overshadow the good that is in them. They understand their strengths and acknowledge their weaknesses. They execute their assignments in a manner that allows their strengths to shine whilst limiting the negative impact of their weaknesses. Over time, they reinforce their strengths through mastery and overcome their weaknesses through self-improvement or total delegation. These are strategies that you can also learn through coaching and mentorship.

HISTORICAL AND CULTURAL BARRIERS TO CONFIDENCE

- *The Legacy of Patriarchy and Colonialism*

If it's so easy to expose self-doubt as a liar and exaggerator as we have just done in the last two paragraphs, the question becomes, why is it equally as easy for us as women to buy into the lies? Whilst the answers to this question might be unique based on the individual experiences of each woman, I believe that most of them share some common threads of our shared experiences. Throughout the history of the human race, women have always been treated as second-class citizens in comparison to men. Viewed as only being fit for maintaining the upkeep of the home and raising kids, we were excluded from participating in countless other facets of society.

This form of patriarchy reigned supreme until the 1700s and 1800s, when women in Europe and the United States of America, respectively, started fighting for the right to vote and own property. After many decades of struggle, women in Finland were eventually granted the right to vote and stand for public office in 1906. After this period, more European countries followed suit, with the majority doing so after World War II in 1945. In the United States of America, women won the right to vote in 1920, but just as in Europe, this did not automatically lead to equality in other areas.

Women still faced exclusion from the workplace, with society believing that they could not do the jobs that men could do. This, by the way, was not based on evidence at all. It was pure arbitrary discrimination born out of the need to keep men superior to women and maintain the societal order of the day. Up until the 1900s, myths such as craniology, a pseudoscience that supposedly proved that men were smarter than women because of their larger brain size, were used to perpetuate this patriarchy and exclude women from institutions such as universities.

It took the extreme events of World War I and World War II for women in the Western world to be allowed to showcase their talents and abilities in the workforce. With men occupied with military activities, women had to fill the gaps in industry, essential services, and public services. These short periods in time enabled those women to change ill-informed perceptions concerning their abilities and the rights they deserved as contributing members of society. It is, however, sad to note that when these wars ended, women were again sidelined to make space for men to work. Even those who were working the same jobs as men did not get paid equally. The attitude of society was that these women were mere placeholders, whose contributions were not needed for post-war economic prosperity.

Aggrieved, these women found themselves on a new battlefield, fighting for recognition and economic inclusion. Inasmuch as this story is difficult to digest, it is just a glimpse of the struggle for equality that women across the world have gone through. This is because it's a story of free European and American White women. Here in Africa, Black women have had to suffer additional discrimination and exclusion based on race. Before we could even think about gender equality, we first had to fight for self-determination and racial equality, due to the chains of colonialism that bound us. This is true for women of colour in the United States of America and Europe who also faced racial discrimination. Women in other parts of the world, including White women in colonial Africa, also faced discrimination unique to the patriarchal systems in their societies.

As African women, not only did we bear the indignity and pain of colonialism, but we also bore the brunt of the gender oppression that came from patriarchy. We were second-class citizens in a second-class society. It has been several decades since most African countries, including Namibia, gained their independence, so one might wonder what relevance this colonial past still has when it comes to women being especially susceptible to self-doubt. Simply put, the answer lies in the enduring legacy of colonialism and patriarchy, which is still felt in corporate Namibia and across Africa. More than that, it still lives on in the everyday experiences of many – if not most – women on the African continent today.

Although our society has come a long way through education, social advocacy, and legal reforms, patriarchal undertones that value the boy over the girl child still exist. In some families, having boys is still celebrated more than having girls. These values create an environment where women are more likely to question their worth and doubt their abilities by default. As I mentioned earlier, self-doubt will prevent you from seeing yourself as capable of success in anything, let alone as a boardroom executive.

VOICES OF STRENGTH: INSIGHTS FROM NAMIBIAN WOMEN

To better understand how this legacy of colonialism and patriarchy impacts women's dreams to occupy the boardroom, I interviewed ten high-powered women executives in corporate Namibia. To protect their identities and the integrity of the institutions that they currently work for or have worked for in the past, I decided not to use their real names. What is key is for us to learn from their stories. Let me introduce you to some of them.

Candice, a seasoned executive with over 25 years of experience in the Namibian Financial Sector and multiple Master's degrees, shared her journey:

> *"As a female leader, I encountered challenges that were often subtle yet deeply impactful. These hurdles were not solely due to my gender but also my race, particularly as a Black woman navigating what was perceived as a predominantly male domain early in my career."*

Her experience highlights the intersection of gender and race as a key factor in the obstacles she faced – an enduring legacy of colonialism and patriarchy. The fact that these challenges were *subtle* suggests they were deeply embedded in the culture of her organisation, so normalised that they were difficult to identify or challenge. Speaking out would have been a risk; without concrete evidence, she could easily have been dismissed or labelled a troublemaker.

Describing these barriers as *deeply impactful* underscores their far-reaching effects. They were not just professional roadblocks but also personal struggles, undermining her confidence and creating self-doubt. The need to *navigate* a male-dominated space indicates that she needed to plan her path carefully, as it was unfamiliar territory.

Candice further reflected: "*Even when I was more qualified, I witnessed my less-qualified White colleagues being empowered and included in key decisions.*" This mirrors the historical struggles of women in Europe and the United States – blatant, arbitrary discrimination designed to uphold racial and patriarchal dominance. Despite her expertise, Candice was systematically sidelined, a stark reminder of the persistent biases that continue to shape corporate spaces today.

Kendra, also a seasoned executive with over 14 years of experience in Namibia's financial sector, reflected on her journey:

> "*One of the greatest challenges I have faced as a female leader is gaining acceptance Earning the recognition and respect of both my male counterparts and subordinates has not always been easy, especially in environments dominated by a 'brotherhood gang' mentality, where I often struggled to be fully included in conversations. As a newly appointed leader, I encountered resistance and subtle undermining from some subordinates who treated my leadership differently than they would have if I were a man.*"

Her experience highlights the ingrained biases that persist in professional spaces, where women in leadership must overcome not only competency expectations but also deep-seated cultural perceptions of authority and belonging.

Beverly is a seasoned executive with 20 years of experience in Namibia's financial sector and the non-bank financial industry. She described experiences that, like Kendra's, were designed to undermine her authority and strip her power as "microaggressions and gaslighting." The subtle resistance these two women faced constituted psychological warfare designed to get them to question their judgement, abilities, and qualities as leaders.

In addition to being subjected to toxic behaviours, these women were also subjected to leadership-limiting cultural expectations. Coming from cultures where women are expected to follow the leadership of men, young women often downplay their position to avoid intimidating male peers. As a result, they may hold back and struggle to fully assert their authority. In this regard, Candice shared, *"Navigating the role of a young manager presented its own set of challenges. Initially, lacking confidence hindered my ability to assert myself and voice my opinions."*

Dantagos, an executive with over 21 years of experience in the financial sector, also highlighted the challenge of balancing ambition with perception, emphasising the need to avoid appearing *too* ambitious. She shared:

> *"Overcoming self-inhibition proved to be a significant challenge for me as a female leader. I found myself grappling with the perspective through which I viewed myself, as well as the lens through which society perceived me. There was a delicate balance to navigate – a desire to pursue ambitions and goals while being careful not to appear overly ambitious. I often questioned whether*

I truly deserved a seat at the table, grappling with limiting thoughts that I had to confront and overcome."

Her poignant insights reveal the tightrope women walk, reconciling external expectations and pressures against inner truth and potential.

Navigating elder respect with the need to assert oneself as a leader was another cultural limitation highlighted in the interviews. Hatagos, a seasoned executive and multi-industry expert who worked her way up from a clerical position, shared her experience on this matter. She recalled:

"Being a young African female leader, it was difficult to understand the unspoken dynamics in meetings and boardrooms, especially if you haven't worked with people collaboratively. It was challenging to collaborate with people who were older than me and contribute fully, so I would find myself not articulating responses because I didn't want to upset the older person. Culturally, we are taught to respect elders, and navigating that cultural element was a bit uncomfortable in the beginning. It took time to find that voice or that blend to be able to contribute to the team and have your ideas heard and spoken in a way that's respectful to everybody but allows you to also participate in the task."

Hatagos' narrative reveals how women are expected to toe the line and devise tactics to contribute in a manner that does not bruise any male or elder egos. This is a skill that male counterparts are less likely to need.

A prominent feature of the colonial and patriarchal legacy is the lack of female representation at the executive level. Beverly explained how being dramatically outnumbered activated feelings of exclusion and perceptions of not belonging, both for her and others. She shared how this historical structure reinforced feelings of marginalisation and self-doubt:

> "*The financial sector of Namibia is a male-dominated industry. In the early stages of my career, often when looking around the table, I've either been the only woman or one of a max of three women. Women are often in the minority in terms of gender.*"

Working in the financial sector as an executive, Given has over 25 years of experience. She recalls:

> "*I was young when I moved into a management position, and I lacked the confidence to execute my duties. The boardrooms were male-dominant environments, which made me uncomfortable, but I navigated it, though it was very tough.*"

Another dream blocker revealed by some of the women in the group was imposter syndrome. In my view, second-guessing one's abilities, downplaying achievements, and feelings of being a fraud or undeserving are all products of the institutional and societal biases against women that we've identified above.

Zoey, an expert in the Namibian financial sector, shared her experience of feeling continual pressure to prove her worth in her role:

> "*I feel fortunate to be pursuing my career during a period when women's empowerment and female leadership are celebrated. However, alongside this progress comes heightened expectations for women to excel and continually prove their worth in their positions. There's a noticeable pressure for women to go above and beyond to demonstrate the deservingness of their roles.*"

With 13 years of local and international experience in the financial sector, Batseba recalls doubters questioning her competency and casting aspersions on the legitimacy of her promotion, despite her tangible accomplishments. She explains,

> *"Upon my promotion to an executive leadership role, doubts were cast on my competencies, and my appointment was scrutinised. To combat these doubts, I had to go above and beyond, investing extra effort into furthering my education to prove my worth to society."*

Last but not least, the final dream blocker subtly impacting women's self-worth and instilling self-doubt is pay disparity. Although Namibia has come a long way in advancing gender parity, compensation gaps persist, indicating lingering biases. Hatagos observes,

> *"Some institutions in Namibia are led by competent female leaders. However, pay equity is still a challenge – male leaders get paid more than female leaders."*

As we have exposed in this chapter, the barriers that we face as women are significant, but they are not insurmountable. Continuing the struggle started by brave women in the 1700s, we will not be stopped in our quest to break into the boardroom and all other leadership spheres of life.

SUMMARY: IDENTIFY AND ELIMINATE THE DREAM BLOCKERS

The stories shared by these Namibian women reveal a recurring theme of strength, resilience, and determination in the face of deeply embedded societal and institutional obstacles. Their voices bring to light the "dream blockers" – subtle yet persistent barriers rooted in colonial legacies, patriarchal structures, racial bias, cultural expectations, imposter syndrome, and gender pay disparities.

Despite being highly qualified, many of these women faced resistance, exclusion, and psychological challenges designed to undermine their confidence and authority. From navigating male-dominated boardrooms and cultural respect dynamics to fighting for recognition and equal compensation, their experiences expose the multifaceted nature of leadership for women in Namibia.

Yet, through each narrative emerges a powerful truth: these challenges, while formidable, are not immovable. Their journeys offer invaluable lessons in courage, self-awareness, and perseverance. As we amplify these voices of strength, we are reminded that representation matters, support systems matter, and that breaking into the boardroom is not just a personal victory, but a collective step forward for all women.

CHAPTER 3
THE FOUNDATION OF LEADERSHIP SUCCESS

"Your career will only grow as far as your belief in your abilities allows."

According to the late Stanford University psychology professor Albert Bandura, self-efficacy is an individual's belief in their capacity to complete tasks and overcome challenges. As a woman aspiring to break into the boardroom, this belief is not just important – it is the foundation of your leadership potential.

Self-efficacy is the internal conviction that you can overcome dream blockers, step into executive roles, and deliver results in high-stakes environments. It is, in my view, the single most important determinant of your career advancement. Why? Because it directly influences how you perceive your capabilities.

As you journey towards the boardroom, you will encounter doubters – some may even be people you respect. That's to be expected. But what you cannot afford is to internalise those doubts or become their source. Once you begin to undermine your abilities, success becomes nearly impossible. Just as you cannot live beyond the quality of your thoughts, you cannot rise in your career beyond the level of your self-efficacy.

UNDERSTANDING SELF-EFFICACY

Self-efficacy is what gives you the audacity to dream big. Women with high self-efficacy are more likely to set ambitious goals and pursue leadership roles. It is the fuel needed to reach the boardroom. Without it, the boardroom remains a distant fantasy. It influences how you identify opportunities and whether you ultimately pursue them.

Low self-efficacy kills ambition. It creates invisible ceilings – self-imposed boundaries to keep you out of spaces you subconsciously believe you don't belong in. Over time, this results in stagnation, regression, and disillusionment.

One powerful example is Ngozi Okonjo-Iweala, who overcame multiple setbacks to become the first African and first woman to lead the World Trade Organization. Despite immense scrutiny and gender-based pushback, her self-efficacy helped her push through. She stated:

> *"If you want to accomplish anything, you must believe in yourself and your abilities."*

Not seeing prospects for growth in your career can lead to job dissatisfaction and demotivation. The job becomes a means to a pay check instead of a source of purpose. It makes the employment relationship purely transactional, and eventually, you may find yourself doing only the bare minimum. That, in turn, may put you in a bad light with an employer who expects you to go over and above the call of duty.

But there's more at stake than just perception. If you stop seeing yourself as making a meaningful contribution to your company, it can negatively impact your self-worth. A lowered self-worth is fertile ground for self-doubt, which can further erode your belief in your abilities. This becomes a vicious circle.

WHAT HIGH SELF-EFFICACY WILL DO FOR YOU

Self-efficacy has been described as the hallmark of effective leadership. It doesn't just ignite your leadership ambitions – it equips you with the traits to realise them.

1. Resilience: The Backbone of Self-Efficacy

Every leader that you admire for their significant accomplishments has had to overcome challenges. If that weren't true, their success would be ordinary and far less meaningful. Like your heroes, high self-efficacy helps you to stay resilient in the face of opposition. What's important to understand about most ambitious goals is that they are not bad ideas; they just need the right conditions to be achieved. Creating these conditions sometimes takes a long time and involves multiple course corrections along the way. Ambitious goals will often be met with resistance, but the leaders who emerge victorious are those who refuse to quit. A high sense of self-efficacy will help you trust in the process, knowing that success often lies on the other side of discomfort.

Indra Nooyi, former CEO and Chair of PepsiCo, often speaks of the resilience required to climb the corporate ladder as a woman of colour. "When you assume leadership, it's not just about you anymore – it's about lifting others too," she said.

This mindset is sustained by resilience, which is powered by self-efficacy.

- *A Personal Journey*

On a personal note, public speaking has become a big part of my coaching and consulting business. Over the years, I have accepted invitations to speak to diverse groups of people, both locally and internationally. From school children to professionals in large corporations, to groups that included high-powered government officials, public speaking has brought me so much joy and fulfilment.

What you may find interesting is that I turned down nearly all my early public speaking opportunities because of fear. The fear of speaking in front of people was such a big challenge to me that I never considered it as an opportunity. I had subconsciously set a boundary against occupying this space, and I did not even know it. Increasing my self-efficacy in this area allowed me to push through the fear and overcome it through preparation and practice. With each speaking engagement, my confidence grew and the fear that once held me back gradually lost its grip – until, through consistent effort and intentional growth, I was finally free of it.

2. Decision-Making: Leading with Clarity and Courage

Self-efficacy has the power to sharpen your decision-making and problem-solving skills. Believing that you can implement your decisions successfully and overcome any resulting challenges improves your decision-making process. This is because you're less likely to be held back by the fear of failure. Without that fear, you can make well-reasoned, fact-based decisions grounded in a realistic assessment of risk.

Leaders with high self-efficacy understand that challenges are constant. Those who embrace problem-solving don't default to the easiest or safest options just to avoid failure. They're also known to be more emotionally regulated, which reduces the likelihood of making impulsive decisions. As such, they are less prone to overestimating benefits or underestimating risks.

"I never lose. I either win or learn." – Nelson Mandela

This quote, embraced by many women leaders, reflects the mindset of leaders with high self-efficacy: every decision holds value, even in failure.

Being confident in your abilities also protects you from analysis paralysis and procrastination – two behaviours that are often linked to a deep fear of failure. Procrastination can give temporary relief and a false sense of control over the problem, but in reality, it only postpones decision-making and compounds stress as deadlines approach.

Confidence in your decision-making removes the need to follow the crowd. Insecure leaders often make poor decisions simply because those choices are popular with the majority. This behaviour is usually driven by fear of judgement if things go wrong, and a need for people's approval. It can serve such leaders for a while, but ultimately, they will be revealed as lacking vision and strength. Organisations don't want people-pleasers – they're looking for mavericks who can inspire and take them to new heights of performance and success. A strong sense of self-efficacy will help you become that kind of leader.

- *The Value of Problem Solvers*

Strong problem-solving abilities will also make you a great candidate for a boardroom promotion. Problem solvers are the most valuable individuals in any corporate organisation because they provide solutions. One of the biggest observations that I made early on in my career is that problems are a constant in the world of business. There is always something that needs fixing – whether it's providing a solution to your client's problem or resolving internal day-to-day operational issues. The individuals who step up to become solution centres for these problems are the ones who make it and thrive in the corporate boardroom.

If you expect things to go smoothly and according to plan all the time, then the boardroom is not for you. The simple reason is that such a utopia does not exist. Problem avoidance is usually a sign of low self-efficacy driven by a lack of belief in one's ability to overcome the challenge.

So the first step in becoming a great problem solver is increasing your self-efficacy. Once the belief is established and good decision-making tools are engaged, problem-solving becomes second nature.

3. Self-Drive and Emotional Regulation: The Fuel of Leadership

Leadership begins from within – it flows from the inside out. You can't lead others effectively if you haven't first learned to lead yourself. And there are no shortcuts.

One of the key ways self-efficacy benefits aspiring leaders like you is by strengthening self-regulation – the ability to manage your thoughts, emotions, and behaviours in a way that aligns with your goals.

Self-regulation includes

- Self-awareness: Knowing who you are, your triggers, and your motivators.
- Self-reflection: Assessing whether your actions align with your values.
- Self-monitoring: Adjusting your behaviour based on feedback and goals.
- Self-drive: Sustaining passion, motivation, and initiative even when challenges arise.

Together, these components shape emotionally intelligent, grounded leaders.

Building self-regulation is only the beginning – the next step is learning to actively manage your emotions so they support, rather than hinder, your leadership journey.

I believe the first step in leading yourself is knowing who you are. You cannot lead what you do not understand. Self-awareness gives you insight into who you are and why you behave the way you do. It shines a light on your motivations, values, thoughts, feelings, beliefs, character, and actions.

One clinical psychologist defines self-awareness as the recognition of one's emotional state at any given moment. Wow. This is profound. Emotions are fleeting, influenced by both our internal experiences and our external environments. As a woman leader, staying aware of your emotions helps you to stay true to yourself. This is where self-awareness and self-reflection work hand in hand. The ability to identify and rectify negative emotions ensures that you always act in ways that align with your values. That alignment keeps your sense of purpose intact and enhances your job satisfaction.

Furthermore, when you're emotionally balanced, your inner peace and harmony will also be reflected in your teams, enhancing your leadership abilities.

Before we move on, it's important to remember that you won't always get it right. Sometimes you will act from a place of negative emotion, and that's okay. When that happens, don't be too hard on yourself. Extend yourself some grace, self-reflect, and correct.

For our purposes, we can define self-reflection as the process of evaluating whether your actions, thoughts, feelings, beliefs, and character align with your values. In my view, mastering your emotions requires constant self-reflection. It's not a once-off exercise reserved for when disaster strikes, but an everyday tool for continuous course correction and personal growth.

Self-reflection is also important in times of success. It helps you identify what's working for you – emotionally, behaviourally, and in your decision-making – so that you can build on those strengths going forward.

A lack of self-drive and leadership are impossible roommates. You cannot be promoted into the boardroom without self-drive. Drive speaks of initiative, motivation, enthusiasm, and passion – all qualities that must come from within. As a leader, it's your responsibility to generate these traits within yourself, without relying on anyone else in your organisation. That is the nature of leadership; the buck stops with you, as we discussed in Chapter 1.

You cannot rely on your superiors or subordinates to provide your drive. As the captain of the ship, your team is looking to you for vision, direction, guidance, inspiration, and excitement. Maintaining self-drive is a big responsibility that you cannot afford to neglect. If you do, you risk your team becoming directionless, demotivated, apathetic, confused, unconfident, and uninspired.

Drive is energy – it's easily transferable and contagious. This is why you have to always show up with your drive at its best. Your energy sets the tone for your entire team.

If you were here now, I am sure you'd say, "Estelle, how is this even possible? Life has its ups and downs. I'm human! How am I expected to always be motivated and enthusiastic? Why should I be held responsible for how other adults feel?"

I know it's a tall order, and I understand why you would feel overwhelmed with this responsibility. But here's the good news – it is possible to maintain self-drive, regardless of the circumstances you're going through.

From the very definition of self-drive, it's apparent that it is largely influenced by your emotions. When you're in a good place emotionally, you are likely to be highly motivated and enthusiastic. Happiness, love, hope, excitement, and contentment inspire a positive outlook and, in turn, fuel self-drive. Conversely, emotions like sadness, fear, anger, anxiety, loneliness, and frustration promote a negative outlook, draining your drive.

As we discussed earlier, the tools of self-awareness and self-reflection are key to regulating your emotional state. This means we have the power to control our emotions and, consequently, our drive. By consciously nurturing positive emotions whilst working to eliminate negative ones, you will ensure that your self-drive remains high, no matter what challenges you face.

The benefits of self-monitoring for leaders with high self-efficacy cannot be overstated. Self-monitoring can be defined as the ability to track, evaluate, and adjust your thoughts, emotions, and behaviour in various settings to achieve pre-determined goals.

As a leader, the reality is that you are expected to keep a lot of people happy. The most successful organisations are those that can balance the needs of multiple stakeholders – clients, employees, shareholders, communities, unions, and even governments – all of whom may have competing interests.

As a leader, your role is to navigate these dynamics in a way that allows you to maintain peak performance while meeting the expectations of each group. This means each stakeholder has to be satisfied that you respectfully gave due consideration to their interests and put your best foot forward to meet them. This requires flexibility and adaptability – qualities that are sharpened through self-monitoring.

4. Adaptability: The Key to Connecting with Others

In my coaching practice, I sometimes have conversations with career people who are struggling to foster and maintain healthy professional relationships with others. I am sometimes met with resistance when I suggest behaviour adaptation. I hear statements such as,

"This is who I am, they should just deal with it."

"With me, what you see is what you get. I cannot sugarcoat anything; I say it as it is."

"People should just accept who I am. It's take it or leave it with me."

In as much as authenticity is important, rigidity limits leadership potential. An unwillingness to modify behaviour suggests that you are perfect and see no need for improvement. This mindset also fails to take into consideration the genuine feelings of others. This attitude is not just unwise; in my experience, it can seriously limit your career progression.

As mentioned earlier in this book, promotion does not take place in a vacuum. Leadership is not a solo journey. This isn't about becoming a people pleaser; it's about being aware of how people see you. This matters if you are going to be a successful leader. Remember, you need them to believe that following you will move them closer to their own success.

On your journey to the boardroom, always remember that people do not follow you to make *you* great. They follow you because they believe you are their best chance for their prosperity. So ask yourself - how will they choose you if you are not willing to meet them where they are?

5. The Boldness to Confront Gender Stereotypes

Finally, knowing your worth is the first step towards claiming your seat at the table. As a woman, a strong sense of self-efficacy will empower you to push back against gender stereotypes and biases that stand in the way of boardroom access. When you know who you are and what you bring to the table, you're far less likely to allow anyone to diminish or unfairly undermine you.

- *Beverly's Story*

Remember Beverly from Chapter 2? This is what she had to say about the matter:

> *"The challenges were very subtle, but I refused to give my power over to people. As a result, I didn't struggle with things like glass ceilings."*

As a result of being confident in her ability to achieve results and overcome any backlash from standing up to patriarchal tyranny, Beverly was able to smash barriers and rise to senior leadership positions in the organisations that she worked for. It is an unfortunate possibility that some of her female colleagues who lacked the same mental fortitude and firepower may have been restricted by the same invisible barriers.

Our fight as women to claim our places in the seats of power is far from over. Therefore, we have to arm ourselves with the tools self-efficacy provides to overcome those barriers. In the 1890s, Alice Lee – one of the first women to attend London University — had to believe in her intellectual abilities first before she went on to successfully disprove that men were smarter than women simply because of their larger skulls.

I can confidently say that throughout history, it's the women with high self-efficacy who've led revolutions in fields dominated by men, from before Alice Lee to modern leaders like Beverly, who are smashing glass ceilings in boardrooms worldwide. These women succeeded because they believed in themselves even when society did not.

THE FOUR PILLARS OF SELF-EFFICACY

Before I teach you how to develop your self-efficacy, let me show you where it comes from. According to prominent organisational psychology researchers, professors Timothy A. Judge and Joyce E. Bono, there are four primary sources of self-efficacy.

1. Personal Experiences

Past successes and failures significantly shape self-efficacy. If you've previously succeeded at a task, you're more likely to believe in your ability to do it again – and to handle any challenges that come with it. The opposite is also true. Failing at a task diminishes your confidence in your ability to succeed the next time that you are faced with something similar. Repeated failure, in particular, can entrench feelings of inadequacy and lead to a significant drop in self-efficacy. This may become an ongoing psychological battle that can be difficult to overcome without coaching interventions.

2. Vicarious Learning

There is no doubt that seeing others succeed in a task that you are about to take on increases your belief that you can do it too, and overcome any challenges along the way. A fascinating example of vicarious learning is seen in what's commonly referred to as the "Roger Bannister effect."

On 6 May 1954, British athlete Roger Bannister became the first person to run a mile in under four minutes, finishing in 3 minutes, 59.4 seconds. Before that, many believed that it was physically impossible, and many mocked the athlete for having such an audacious goal. It took him two years of training to eventually succeed.

What is mind-blowing about the story is that just 46 days later, Australian runner John Landy – Bannister's rival – beat the record by running the mile in 3 minutes 58.0 seconds. The following year, three athletes ran a sub-4-minute mile in the same race, and many others have done the same since then.

The question is, how did Landy and the others break the 4-minute mile when they had failed to do so before Bannister? The answer lies in vicarious learning. Seeing Roger Bannister succeed gave them belief and sparked self-efficacy. His breakthrough proved it could be done and gave them the confidence that they could do it too.

Conversely, just as with personal experiences, observing repeated failure in others who you believe have similar abilities can diminish your self-efficacy. This can lead to an unhealthy pattern of internalising those failures as your own. You might even start thinking or saying statements such as, "People like me do not achieve much." These limiting beliefs are not based on facts, but on a distorted view shaped by repeated negative examples.

3. Social Persuasion

Receiving feedback and encouragement can positively influence self-efficacy. Studies have shown that female leaders who received positive feedback from their mentors, coaches, and peers exhibited higher self-efficacy in leadership roles. While this is a valuable source of motivation, over-reliance on it can lead to unintended results. Sometimes, positive feedback and words of encouragement from others do not come, and excessive dependence on the proverbial "pat on the back" can lead to unhealthy patterns of seeking approval, leading to reduced decision-making ability. Conversely, a leader doing a great job may still be the recipient of unfair criticism. Relying too much on feedback and encouragement in such situations can lead to reduced confidence and lowered self-efficacy. As such, you must learn how to self-validate and maintain confidence, even in the absence of recognition.

4. Physiological and Emotional States

Leadership is a high-pressure environment. The demands of a senior position combined with historical patriarchal biases can lead to stress and self-doubt, ultimately reducing self-efficacy. Managing these emotional and physiological states is essential to maintain belief in your abilities. Furthermore, other negative experiences cause self-doubt in women. Being part of a historically vulnerable group has resulted in a significant number of women carrying emotional trauma on their journey to the boardroom.

Unresolved trauma is a stumbling block to leadership, one that cannot be avoided. The more it's hidden, the more likely it is to resurface at the most inconvenient times, further reducing self-efficacy and causing untold damage. In the next chapter, we explore how to take back your self-worth and ultimately grow your self-confidence. I look forward to guiding you on this journey.

SUMMARY: SELF-EFFICACY – YOUR GATEWAY TO THE BOARDROOM

Self-efficacy is more than just a personal belief – it is the bedrock of transformational leadership. It empowers you to dream big, take bold action, navigate challenges, and lead with authenticity and purpose. Without it, the journey to the boardroom is filled with hesitation and missed opportunities. With it, no barrier is too high, no stereotype too powerful, and no setback too final.

From building resilience and making sound decisions to mastering emotional regulation and confronting gender bias, self-efficacy gives you the internal strength required to thrive in high-level leadership. It allows you to break invisible boundaries, silence self-doubt, and position yourself as a solution-driven, emotionally intelligent leader the boardroom cannot ignore.

As you move forward, remember that self-efficacy can be cultivated. It is strengthened through experience, inspired by others, encouraged by positive feedback, and maintained through emotional well-being. This chapter has shown you that the power to lead starts within. Believe you belong – because you do. The boardroom is not reserved for the chosen few. It's waiting for you to claim your seat.

CHAPTER 4
BUILDING UNSHAKEABLE CONFIDENCE

"You cannot expect others to have confidence in you if you do not have confidence in yourself."

In 2021, I published *The 30-Day Self-Confidence Journal* in response to what I discovered to be a dire need for self-confidence coaching amongst women in corporate Namibia. Before this, I had organised a group coaching workshop with ten women, and all of them wanted coaching on self-confidence. I thought to myself, "If all ten of these brilliant women want self-confidence coaching, surely there are many others like them battling with similar challenges." The incredible response to the journal confirmed my suspicion, with nearly 2000 copies sold to date.

As a woman who wants to break into the boardroom, you need to understand that self-confidence is the foundation of self-efficacy. Whilst self-efficacy is your belief in your ability to complete a specific task and overcome challenges, self-confidence is the overall trust that you have in your qualities, judgement, and abilities.

THE BENEFITS OF SELF-CONFIDENCE

Self-confidence is an absolute necessity for living a happy and fulfilled life. It benefits both your career and personal life, and as a woman, it is also great for your well-being. Knowing that you can trust in your qualities, judgement, and abilities to achieve the goals that you set for yourself is both empowering and uplifting. Self-confidence doesn't just help you dream big; it also gives you the courage to pursue the best that your career and life have to offer.

As a woman leader, your self-confidence positions you for a boardroom promotion. Influence is the currency of leadership, and self-confidence is the magnet that attracts it. When you have confidence in yourself, others will have confidence in you. We all want to be led by confident people. Just look at all the people that you consider to be mentors or role models in the areas of life where you want to succeed. They are all confident. You wouldn't follow someone who doesn't project confidence in their ability. Even if their direction turns out to be wrong, their confidence is what makes you follow them.

Confidence positions you as a strong candidate for leadership opportunities. It is not just your subordinates who need to believe in you, the same goes for your superiors as well. For them to trust you with responsibility, they need to see you as the right woman for the job. Leadership flows in the direction of self-confidence. When you're confident, you become more visible, more likely to raise your hand, and more willing to take responsibility when solutions are needed.

This kind of proactive behaviour will give you a reputation as a leader who can be relied upon when the going gets tough. And that's exactly the type of reputation that you need to put you on the fast track to the boardroom. Remember, perception informs influence. The more decision makers you impact positively, the more likely you are to earn a vote of confidence when it's time for promotion.

Self-confidence further enhances your personal and professional life by empowering you to communicate boldly and assertively. The ability to speak directly and honestly without any fear of reprisal is the key to successful relationships. Not only does effective communication aid your relationships, but it also helps you achieve your goals.

Most of the significant goals that we set for ourselves, including breaking into the boardroom, require the cooperation of others. This means we need to be able to communicate our requirements effectively to them. With self-confidence, you won't feel the urge to be passive or aggressive – you will be able to communicate in a way that satisfactorily conveys your needs. Assertive communication not only promotes harmonious relationships within your circle of influence, but also builds more confidence within you.

Self-confidence also helps you create and maintain boundaries that protect your self-worth or values. People with high self-confidence tend to have a strong sense of self-worth, which enables them to set high standards for how they expect others to treat them. They quickly recognise demeaning, toxic behaviour from others – whether personally or professionally – and have the courage to stand up for themselves when necessary. They are not afraid to teach others how to treat them.

Furthermore, self-confidence enhances clarity around your values. When you trust your judgement and know who you are, you're less likely to second-guess yourself or act in ways that go against what you believe in. This inner clarity also buffers you against pressure from others who may try to coerce or deceive you into acting against your values.

Those who lack self-confidence are more likely to compromise their values for the sake of convenience or approval. They are afraid to walk away when faced with disadvantage or ridicule. In your quest to break into the boardroom, you want to be known as a principled and uncompromising leader who always stands for what is right. This will not only increase your self-respect but also increase your influence amongst others, setting you up for greater leadership responsibility.

Finally, although by no means exhaustively, self-confidence also enables you to accept constructive criticism with grace. Self-confident people are secure in themselves, so they don't take it personally when others point out what they could be doing better. Self-confidence empowers you to draw from the strength that lies in humility. When you're chasing a big dream, such as breaking into the boardroom, wisdom correctly tells you that you do not know everything.

Often, we are unconsciously incompetent, meaning that we are unaware of the gaps in our knowledge or skills. That's why you need people around you to equip you with the skills that you need to perform at a high level. You also need others who will help you with identifying your weaknesses and potential pitfalls that may lie along your journey. One powerful lesson that I have learned in life is this: every person I encounter has something valuable to teach me. It does not matter their age, status, or level of education – everyone has a lesson for you. That is the beauty of our human connection, and it is self-confidence that helps us access that shared wisdom.

Always remember that it is not a weakness to not know something. No one expects their leader to have all the answers.

What is expected from a leader is to be open and willing to learn and apply that knowledge to achieve set goals.

As you can see, just like self-efficacy, self-confidence is a non-negotiable weapon to have in your arsenal when aiming for the boardroom. At this point, you might be saying to yourself, "That rules me out, then. I was not born with self-confidence, so I might as well quit on this dream of conquering the boardroom." If that's you, I have great news for you. There is no need for you to quit because self-confidence is a skill set that you can develop. This means everyone, including you, can become self-confident. It is not something that is reserved for a select few who have life perfectly figured out. With the right coaching and support, you can build your self-confidence, and I am now going to show you three simple ways to do so.

1. Silence the Noise

"When there is no enemy within, the enemy outside cannot harm." – African Proverb

When it comes to self-confidence, the "enemy" is anything or anyone that causes you to lose trust in your abilities, judgement, or qualities. In other words, it is anything that fuels self-doubt. To bring it closer to home, this enemy could be you, other people, or your surrounding circumstances. When it comes from others or your environment, it's external noise. But when you internalise it, it becomes internal noise – and that's when it truly starts to chip away at your confidence.

The beauty of this proverb is that it tells us that if you are strong and grounded within yourself, no outside influence can diminish your self-confidence. This is awesome because it means *you* are the one in control. There is no one else who can sabotage your self-belief or let you down.

Another interesting fact that you need to know is that you can never stop the enemy outside from coming against you – whether it's criticism, rejection, or tough circumstances. But you can control the effect it has on you, and this is your true defence. What do I mean by this? For example, you cannot stop people from doubting you, but you can stop their doubts from clouding your judgement. You cannot stop your country's economy from declining, but you *can* choose to be resourceful and prosper.

- *Manifestations of Internal Noise*

Internal noise often shows up as a negative inner voice that I call the inner bully. If left unchecked, this bully can be the biggest enemy of progress in your life. The inner bully not only destroys your self-confidence, but also amplifies your doubts and fears. It paralyses you and prevents you from doing tasks that you are fully capable of completing. It also holds you back in life and stops you from pursuing your dreams.

So, how do you know if this bully is present in your life? Well, it is easy to identify. It's the voice inside your head that whispers things like, "I am not good enough. I am not smart enough. I am not attractive. I am worthless. My voice is irrelevant. I am a failure. I will never amount to much. I will never catch a good break."

The inner bully is truly the voice of negative affirmations, and the louder it gets, the more self-doubt takes hold. If it's not stopped, these messages start to shape your thinking. They begin to form patterns of limiting thoughts and beliefs. Before you know it, you will have cultivated a full-blown negative self-perception that destroys your self-confidence.

That is the danger of the inner bully: it creates an invisible ceiling on your personal and professional progression. This can even lead to regression because your life flows in the direction of your most dominant thoughts.

- *Sources of Internal Noise*

The interesting aspect of internal noise is that no one is born with it. None of us entered the world filled with self-doubt. In fact, the opposite is true – we were all born with self-confidence. Just look at how we behave when we first come into this world as infants. The first thing that we do is demand attention by letting out a loud cry. From there on, we cry, urgently demanding milk, cuddles, and diaper changes without any room for negotiation. We are so confident of getting what we want that we even increase the decibels of our cries if we experience any delays, regardless of what our caregiver is doing.

As we grow into toddlers, we maintain the same level of self-confidence, believing that we can do anything. Even powerful forces like gravity do not exist for us. It is only when we start hearing and internalising the word *no* that our self-confidence begins to diminish. All of a sudden, we begin to realise that not all things are possible or permissible. This is when we allow the external noise to become internal noise. In other words, internal noise often starts on the outside – it's shaped by the messages we hear and absorb from the world around us.

Some common forms of external noise include:

- *Systematic Patriarchal Biases*

In Chapter 2, we discussed how systematic patriarchal biases designed to keep women as a sub-category of the human race ultimately eroded women's sense of self-worth. Unfortunately, without the right mental fortitude, anyone who is constantly undervalued can begin to see themselves as valueless. In my opinion, this history and its lingering remnants have made women susceptible to the effects of the other forms of external noise below. That is why women generally face more self-confidence challenges than men.

The Mute Button

As established previously, the only way to mute the noise of systematic patriarchal biases is by confronting them. There is no reason why women should be treated as inferior to men. Never allow such prejudice to go unchallenged in your various spaces of influence. Be bold and stand up for yourself when needed.

- *Hurtful Words and Negative Opinions of Others*

As little children, we used to sing, "Sticks and stones can break my bones, but words can never hurt me." This could not have been further from the truth. Words are powerful. They either build or destroy. They can enter the subconscious mind and give birth to beliefs that can last a lifetime. Unfortunately, many women have been subjected to hurtful words from acquaintances and loved ones alike. Hurtful words from trusted and esteemed sources such as parents, teachers, bosses, and spouses have left many with debilitating self-doubt.

The Mute Button

Developing a strong mind is critical for muting the noise of hurtful words and negative opinions of others. Remember, you cannot stop people from having negative opinions about you or saying hurtful words to you. What you *can* stop is accepting these opinions and words as truth and internalising them. Freeing yourself from the need for validation is an offshoot of a strong mind that will shield you from the impact of others' hurtful words and negative opinions. If you find yourself in an environment where you are constantly subjected to harmful or belittling language, it's important to speak up. Raise your concerns with the person responsible or escalate them through the appropriate channels. If this fails, you will need to have the courage to remove yourself from that environment to protect your dignity and self-worth.

Quick Exercise

Think back to your earliest memory and write down all the negative words that you recall having been spoken to you or about you. Start with the ones that have been the most impactful over the years. List them down on one side of a page. Now, cross each word out with a line through the middle and next to it, write a positive affirmation that counters the lie. For example, if the negative word is *dumb*, cross it out and write *I am intelligent*. If it was *ugly*, cross it out and write *I am beautiful*. Use this list as often as you can to affirm yourself and bury the lies of the enemy outside forever. Turn the words that were meant to destroy you into affirmations to build your self-confidence. Repeated positive affirmations help create new mental pathways, training your mind to align your life with the truth of who you are.

- *Traumatic Events*

An unfortunate reality of life is that we sometimes experience deeply stressful and frightening experiences that are out of our control. According to the World Health Organization, one in every three women across the globe has experienced some sort of physical violence. That is a staggering 33%!

This kind of violence can cause psychological trauma, leading to feelings of vulnerability, powerlessness, and a diminished sense of worth. Tragic losses and severe illness are also sources of the trauma that some of us carry. In addition to negative emotional states such as anger, bitterness, and unforgiveness, unresolved trauma can lead to severe mental health challenges such as anxiety and depression.

As women, we've learned to be resilient, and we often carry on despite this inner turmoil. But this emotional weight can quietly sabotage our efforts to succeed, whether in the boardroom or any area of life. We have to confront and silence the noise created by the trauma that we have faced.

The Mute Button

Like hurtful words and opinions, the first step towards muting the voice of internal trauma is to acknowledge and confront it. You do not heal trauma by sweeping it under the rug. While facing those painful memories may reopen old wounds, it's the only path to true healing.

A key part of your healing journey is going to be forgiveness. You are going to have to forgive the perpetrators of this trauma, and if you feel guilt or shame for being a victim, it's time to release that too. You are *not* at fault for what happened. Traumatic events occur simply because we are human and we live in this imperfect world.

If, like me, you believe in God, I encourage you to hand your trauma over to Jesus. That is how I have overcome the darkest periods in my life. Lastly, I am not a trauma expert. If you believe you need extra help to process and heal, please seek professional help.

External Environmental Hardships

There is no doubt that we are living in an increasingly difficult and chaotic world. Everywhere we look, there are hardships – major wars, devastating natural disasters, and global unrest – that are turning lives upside down. Here at home, the unemployment rate and cost of living keep climbing. Our communities are also in upheaval due to various societal ills. Things are no longer as they used to be, and this is all external noise that can start creating uncertainty within you. Not knowing what the future holds can be detrimental to our self-confidence as women because we often greatly value stability and security.

The Mute Button

The way to silence the voice of future uncertainties is by forming a positive outlook on life. In my observation and analysis of difficult circumstances, I have realised something powerful – that the sky is never truly falling. No matter how hard things get, there are always people who prosper in the same environment that others find challenging.

You can go to the poorest countries on earth, and you'll still find rich individuals there. Why? Because of their mindset. Empower yourself to strengthen your mindset and continuously set goals that give you momentum when accomplished. Working towards and achieving your goals will give you a sense of direction and purpose, and accomplishing them will further enhance your self-confidence.

2. Overcome Your Fears

Fear stifles self-confidence. When you are overwhelmed with fear, it becomes impossible to trust in your qualities, judgement, or abilities. Fear paralyses you and stops you from achieving your goals. It is the number one killer of dreams and ambition. It's the reason why so many people procrastinate and delay their greatness.

Fear is the opposite of faith. Where faith says, "This could work," fear will convince you that your actions will lead to disaster. The most ironic thing about fear is that its conclusions are often baseless. There is no real evidence behind them. It is the trick of the brain to stop you from stepping outside your comfort zone. Whenever you are faced with fear, remember that your mind and body are creatures of comfort. They enjoy being comfortable and will always oppose being stretched. That's why whenever you consider doing something unfamiliar or challenging, fear shows up to try and stop you.

For example, if you tell yourself you want to start exercising, the first thoughts that come to mind are the possibility of injuring yourself or collapsing from fatigue. Similarly, if you tell yourself you want to learn a new skill, your brain starts telling you that you will fail. This is because it does not want to be challenged. The interesting thing, however, is that once you take that first step in your running shoes, the fear begins to fade. Once you open that textbook or attend that first class, your brain kicks into action and gets into conquering mode. The key? Start anyway. The only way to overcome fear is to move through it – and discover that what's on the other side isn't as scary as you thought.

- **FEAR** *is truly **F**alse **E**vidence **A**ppearing **R**eal.*

Fear not only kills your dreams but also robs you of precious life experiences. Growing up, my parents forbade my siblings and me from swimming in the ocean. I do not know what my parents had experienced to impose that strict rule on us, but they always told us, "There's nothing to hold onto if something goes wrong." As a result, we never learned how to swim – not in the ocean or even a swimming pool. Water became a taboo topic, and unsurprisingly, I developed a deep fear of it.

I know my parents were trying to protect us, and they were doing so out of love. But, unfortunately, I inherited their fear of water to the extent that I would not even attempt to learn how to swim. How irrational is that? If something is beneficial and safe for others, is it not logical to learn how to do it safely rather than avoid it altogether?

But fear doesn't work with logic. It just says, *"Do not do it. If you make any attempts to learn, you will die."* Fear is so irrational that it has been established that up to 91% of the things that we fear never happen. Additionally, of the 9% of things that end up happening, the effects do not turn out as badly as we predicted.

From my book *Breaking Barriers*, you may remember that it took having to undergo physical rehabilitation as an adult for me to learn how to swim in a swimming pool. But the real test came in 2021, during a family holiday in Zanzibar.

We took a boat trip to one of the best snorkelling spots on the ocean, and as usual, I was content to stay on the boat. All of a sudden, my two 14-year-old nieces jumped into the water. I looked at their mother, expecting panic, but she was completely calm. Moments later, *my* two daughters jumped in too. That's when I started praying in tongues!

All manner of thoughts started to run through my mind. *What if something happens to them? What will I tell my mother? How will I respond if she asks me why I let them get into the ocean?* As these thoughts were running through my mind, my 7-year-old niece jumped in as well.

At this point, instead of feeling more fearful, I was challenged. *If a 7-year-old can join these other kids in having fun, what am I doing on this boat?* I asked myself. *Estelle, are you going to allow fear to rob you of this precious moment with your daughters and nieces? How long is this fear going to dominate you?*

At that moment, I drew the line in the sand and decided I was going to join them in the water. I fastened my life jacket and asked the three lifeguards to pay attention to me and to have the floating ring close by. When the kids saw all this commotion, they started cheering me on. I told them to count to three, and as they reached three, I jumped. I faced my fear and won.

Facing your fears head-on is the only way that you will overcome them and build your self-confidence. The more fears you face, the more powerful and confident you become.

Quick Exercise

Make a list of all your fears and write them down one by one. Take a moment to reflect on why you think you have each of these fears. Understanding the source of your fear is important because you cannot conquer what you do not understand. As you list these fears, think about what each one is robbing you of and how important that thing is to you. Fear often holds us back from reaching our full potential or enjoying experiences, so make sure you recognise what's at stake.

Once you've done this, think about how you are going to confront each fear. Action is needed. Fear is not just something you overcome in your mind. You need to step out and push your boundaries. Whether it's speaking out, trying something new, or taking risks, confronting your fears requires you to take action. As you do this, you will break the chains of fear and begin to live life to the fullest.

It's also important to know that you might experience some discomfort. There is always discomfort when you are going against the norm. Some people may even question you, or you might experience physical or emotional pain. Completing new tasks can be challenging, but don't give up. As you gain new skills and competence, it will become easier. It is all part of the process of overcoming fear.

3. Develop Your Skills

It's natural to feel nervous or anxious whenever you try something new. As a result of your attempt, one of two things will happen: you either succeed or fail. When you succeed, you will feel great, and it will boost your confidence. While this once-off success feels great, it doesn't build lasting self-confidence because you haven't yet developed the competence needed for long-term success. It is only after several attempts that you will truly hone your skills and develop lasting self-confidence. Even if you accidentally fail later, once you have developed competence, your self-confidence will not be impacted.

Conversely, when you experience failure on that first attempt, self-doubt can creep in, leading to demotivation and feelings of rejection. This failure can also heighten insecurities and fuel procrastination. The key to avoiding being stuck at this point is to understand that it is okay to fail because it is part of the journey to competence. Accept that you have not yet learned the skill and keep trying until you do. Remember, it is only failure when you quit.

A few years ago, my daughters told me that they wanted to participate in gymnastics. I was a bit taken aback because no one from my family or my husband's family had ever done gymnastics. As a mother who encourages my children to explore their talents and try new things, I agreed to enrol them in a gymnastics club. In their first year, they performed well, reaching the national championships, although they had not honed their skills. My youngest, Kayla, finished fifth, while my eldest, Keasha, obtained a bronze medal, both in their respective categories.

Ever looking for ways to sharpen skills, I noticed that there was one particular club whose girls took most of the medals. So, I decided to switch the girls to that club the following year. That January, we were greeted by a very strict coach who seldom smiled, and for a moment, I thought I had made a mistake. She proceeded to tell us that the girls would not be participating in any competitions for nine months and would be expected to train for two hours a day, from Monday to Friday. The girls happily took on the challenge, even training some Saturdays. During one school holiday they spent two weeks training at the High-Performance Centre in South Africa.

After nine months of this intense training, my daughters began participating in competitions again. They qualified again for the national championships, but this time Kayla won one gold and one silver medal. Keasha earned three golds and one silver and ended up representing Namibia in the regional championships in South Africa, where she won a bronze. Who would have thought that such extraordinary results could be obtained in just one year? This result was not just the passage of time but the focused skill development that took place within that year. It made my girls more competent and significantly bolstered their self-confidence.

SUMMARY: BUILDING UNSHAKEABLE CONFIDENCE

Self-confidence is the foundation of influence, visibility, and leadership. It empowers you to trust in your judgement, stand firm in your values, communicate effectively, and boldly pursue opportunities – even in the face of fear or opposition. As a woman striving for the boardroom, your confidence is not just a nice-to-have; it's a necessity.

The good news is that confidence isn't a fixed trait – it's a skill you can build. By silencing internal and external noise, confronting your fears, and developing your skills, you strengthen your inner trust and position yourself as a leader worth following.

Confidence grows through action. Keep showing up, keep building, and never underestimate the power of believing in yourself.

CHAPTER 5
COACHING AND MENTORSHIP

"Behind every successful woman is a tribe of other successful women who have her back."

In the pursuit of boardroom leadership, technical expertise and professional ambition alone are not enough. The path is often riddled with systemic challenges, unspoken biases, and invisible barriers that require more than talent to overcome. What truly sets successful women leaders apart is not just their qualifications – it's their unshakeable belief in their ability to lead, influence, and create change. This belief is called self-efficacy, and it is the fuel that propels women into positions of power and purpose.

But even the most determined leaders can struggle to sustain this belief when faced with persistent resistance, under-representation, and environments that question their worth. This is why coaching and mentorship are not optional – they are essential. These two pillars of support offer more than encouragement; they provide strategy, perspective, and accountability. They sharpen your edge, elevate your mindset, and fortify your confidence for the journey ahead.

In this chapter, we will explore how coaching and mentorship work in tandem to build resilient, empowered, and self-efficacious women leaders. You will discover how to attract the right guidance, leverage these relationships for growth, and avoid the common pitfalls that derail development. Most importantly, you'll learn that self-efficacy is not just something you feel – it's something you *build*, *practise*, and *own*.

Candice, whose story you encountered in Chapter 2, captures this reality beautifully: "*The guidance and wisdom I've gained from mentoring relationships have propelled my career forward. Additionally, coaching has played a pivotal role in reshaping my approach to leadership, equipping me to navigate corporate hurdles and career challenges with greater efficacy.*"

The boardroom is not beyond your reach. With the right support and the right mindset, it becomes your next destination.

THE VALUE OF COACHING

A coach will not play the game for you, but they will teach you how to play it strategically and effectively. As an executive and transformational coach, my approach is to walk alongside you as a thought partner, engaging in a transformative process that inspires you to unlock your full potential, both personally and professionally. You already possess the raw talent and drive to reach the boardroom, but just as athletes can benefit from coaching, so can you. You are not lacking; you are whole, creative, and resourceful – an expert in your own life and career. Together, we refine your talent and channel it into actionable strategies that lead to exceptional results.

- *The Role of Coaching*

Coaching is a transformative partnership that empowers you to confront real-time challenges with clarity, strategy, and purpose. It provides a structured yet flexible space to set meaningful, career-aligned goals – whether it's sharpening your decision-making, mastering self-regulation, elevating your communication, or becoming a more agile problem solver. These are not just professional competencies – they are the very building blocks of self-efficacy and authentic leadership.

A skilled coach functions as your strategic thought partner, equipping you with tailored tools, honest feedback, and unwavering support. Unlike generic development programmes, coaching meets you where you are and guides you to where you're meant to be. It enables you to convert ambition into action and uncertainty into confident execution.

Each coaching session becomes a catalyst for growth. With every insight gained and milestone achieved, your belief in your ability deepens. This renewed confidence doesn't just prepare you for the next challenge – it positions you to lead it.

Moreover, coaching is not about fixing weaknesses; it's about unlocking potential. It spotlights your strengths, addresses blind spots, and challenges you to stretch beyond your comfort zone. Through intentional guidance and reflective practice, coaching becomes the engine that accelerates your journey to the boardroom – and keeps you thriving once you're there.

- *The Power of Mentorship*

While coaching is a powerful tool, mentorship offers another dimension of support – drawing from the wisdom of those who have already travelled the path you aspire to walk. Unfortunately, mentorship is often misunderstood. Many professionals recognise its value but fail to establish meaningful relationships that yield tangible benefits. A mentor is not your friend, your colleague, or a shortcut to success. They are not obligated to provide you with answers, opportunities, or access to their networks.

True mentorship is a relationship built on respect and shared vision, where an experienced guide helps you navigate challenges, offering insights rooted in lived experience. During my time as a corporate executive, I encountered individuals seeking mentorship for the wrong reasons – some expecting quick promotions or financial support under the guise of mentorship. Similarly, as an entrepreneur running Kauai restaurants, I was approached by those hoping to benefit from my business success for personal gain rather than seeking genuine guidance.

A mentor's role is to provide counsel and guidance in areas where they have already achieved success. This could range from leadership and career advancement advice to personal goals such as wealth creation or health. For mentorship to be effective, two fundamental criteria must be met: First, the mentor must have demonstrable success in the area where you seek guidance. Second, they must be genuinely willing to invest in your growth.

Coaching and mentorship are invaluable tools for building self-efficacy, but they are not shortcuts. They are partnerships that challenge you to step into your full potential, equipping you with the skills, strategies, and confidence to take ownership of your leadership journey. With the right coach and mentor by your side, the boardroom is no longer a distant dream – it becomes an attainable destination.

ATTRACTING THE RIGHT MENTORSHIP

- *Becoming a Magnet for Mentors*

Finding the right mentor begins with clarity about what you need and identifying those who align with your goals. Potential mentors are often easy to spot – they are the leaders who have successfully navigated the boardrooms and industries you aspire to enter. A quick search can reveal a list of accomplished C-suite executives within your organisation, your industry, or even across sectors. These individuals may be male or female, but shared experiences often make female mentors particularly relatable, as they may have faced challenges similar to those you encounter today.

The effectiveness of mentorship, much like coaching, depends on the alignment of societal and organisational contexts. As explored throughout this book, women leaders face unique systemic challenges, particularly in corporate environments. For this reason, I strongly recommend seeking mentors who have first-hand experience overcoming the obstacles you currently face – or those you anticipate encountering on your journey.

Once you identify potential mentors, the next step is establishing their willingness to mentor you. Remember, mentorship is not a casual undertaking. It requires a significant investment of time, energy, and emotional commitment from both parties. Mentors pour their insights and experiences into their mentees without any expectation of material gain. Some even feel a profound sense of responsibility for the success of those they mentor.

This brings us to an important truth: Mentors are attracted, not pursued. While you can initiate a mentorship relationship, the key to success lies in making yourself an attractive mentee. The qualities that draw mentors are rooted in your character, actions, and approach. Here's how you can stand out:

1. A Proven Track Record

Mentors at the C-suite level are drawn to results. Demonstrating your potential through tangible achievements in your current role sends a clear message: you are serious about your career and committed to growth. Begin collecting wins within your area of responsibility, as these successes not only build your reputation but also signal to prospective mentors that you are worth their time and effort.

2. Initiative and Enthusiasm

Mentors value individuals who take initiative. Volunteering for additional responsibilities within your team or organisation is an excellent way to get noticed. Beyond your core duties, participating in non-work-related initiatives such as social impact projects or team-building activities increases your visibility and demonstrates your enthusiasm. Enthusiasm, in particular, is a powerful force – it's contagious and can make you truly irresistible to the right mentor.

3. Shared Ambition

In the workplace, some of the most effective mentor–mentee relationships form naturally within reporting lines. Leaders directly above you in the organisational hierarchy often benefit from your success, making mentorship a mutually advantageous relationship. To leverage this dynamic, take time to understand your prospective mentor's goals and align yourself with their ambitions. Show them that their investment in you will also contribute to their success.

4. Teachability

Teachability is the cornerstone of any successful mentorship relationship. Would-be mentors are naturally drawn to individuals who are open to learning and genuinely humble. Demonstrating a willingness to receive feedback, reflect on guidance, and act on advice is essential. Mentorship is a two-way street, and your openness to growth ensures that the relationship remains dynamic, productive, and fulfilling for both parties.

Securing mentorship is less about pursuing someone to help you and more about positioning yourself as someone they want to support. By building a strong foundation of results, demonstrating initiative, aligning with shared ambitions, and maintaining a teachable spirit, you create opportunities for meaningful mentorship relationships that will propel you towards the boardroom and beyond.

THE SELF-EFFICACY BOOST: WHAT COACHING AND MENTORSHIP UNLOCK

Self-efficacy is the foundation of confident, impactful leadership. For women striving to break into the boardroom, it is not just about believing in your ability to succeed but about reinforcing that belief amid external challenges and internal doubts. Coaching and mentorship serve as transformative tools in this journey, equipping leaders with the clarity, resilience, and skills necessary to navigate complex organisational landscapes.

Through targeted guidance and support, these relationships address the core challenges that undermine self-efficacy, from dismantling imposter syndrome to mastering the art of self-advocacy, and building skills for leadership success. They empower leaders to harness their potential, overcome systemic barriers, and thrive authentically. Here are some guides:

1. Silencing the Doubt: Conquering Imposter Syndrome

Imposter syndrome is one of the most insidious barriers to self-efficacy. It creates a false narrative of inadequacy, even in the face of evident achievements. As a woman, you cannot afford to let this mindset coexist with your leadership aspirations – because they are mutually exclusive. Coaching and mentorship provide a crucial recalibration tool, helping women confront and dismantle these limiting beliefs.

Namibia, like many other countries, has introduced affirmative action policies to address gender disparities in leadership. While these measures have increased female representation, they have also unintentionally triggered feelings of undeservingness in some women. In my interview with executive women leaders, Zoey shared how the pressure to constantly prove her worth as a leader made her feel like she had to "go above and beyond" to validate her place. Similarly, Batseba felt compelled to "pursue additional qualifications" to counter doubts about her leadership competency.

While professional development is commendable, the motive matters. These women were driven not by growth aspirations but by a need to combat the narrative of imposter syndrome – a narrative fuelled by systemic biases. Coaching and mentorship address this at its root, helping women recognise their inherent worth and capabilities. Through guided discussions and constructive feedback, these interventions build self-perception and belief, empowering leaders to focus on results rather than external validation.

The key to defeating imposter syndrome lies in embracing the truth of your qualifications, achievements, and potential. Trust the judgement of those who placed you in positions of responsibility, and remember that your past successes are evidence of your capability. When you focus on delivering results and leading authentically, self-doubt diminishes, and self-efficacy flourishes.

2. Finding Your Voice: The Power of Self-Advocacy

Advocating for yourself as a leader is not optional – it is essential. Yet, for many women, systemic blockers strip away their voices, leaving them feeling silenced and sidelined. Kendra, for example, faced a "brotherhood gang" mentality in her team, making it difficult to assert her authority. Candice echoed similar sentiments, sharing how a *"lack of confidence early in her career hindered her ability to voice her opinions."*

Coaching and mentorship play a pivotal role in restoring that voice. Through these partnerships, leaders learn the art of assertive communication, enabling them to confront discrimination and champion their ideas with confidence. Candice summed it up perfectly: *"Timidity has no place in leadership. One must actively advocate for their seat at the table."*

Self-advocacy requires not just confidence but also strategic communication. Coaching equips leaders with the tools to frame conversations effectively, ensuring that their messages are heard and respected. Mentorship adds another layer of support, offering insights and tactics to navigate difficult conversations while maintaining emotional poise.

Zoey's experience highlights the transformative power of mentorship. *"Mentoring amplified my visibility and enabled me to advocate for myself confidently,"* she shared. By honing her ability to articulate her thoughts effectively, she became a more influential and impactful leader.

Self-advocacy is an ongoing process. As challenges evolve, so must your strategies. With the support of coaching and mentorship, women develop resilience, strategic thinking, and the mental fortitude needed to advocate for themselves and their ideas consistently.

3. Mastering Your Craft: Building Skills for Leadership Success

Skill mastery is the bedrock of exceptional leadership. The stronger your skills, the more your confidence and self-efficacy grow. For women navigating male-dominated spaces, coaching and mentorship are invaluable in honing the critical competencies needed to succeed and lead with authority.

Dantagos provides a compelling example of how mentorship can bridge the gap between theoretical knowledge and practical application. *"Under his mentorship, I gained essential skills not taught in formal education – staying informed on economic developments, mastering time management, and excelling in writing and planning,"* she shared. These newfound competencies not only boosted her confidence but also solidified her reputation as a credible and capable leader in her field.

Batseba also reflected on the transformative power of coaching in enhancing her decision-making abilities – a cornerstone of effective leadership. *"Coaching and mentoring helped me uncover my authentic leadership style, fostering clarity and thoughtful decision-making through reflection and avoiding impulsive choices,"* she noted.

By equipping leaders with real-world insights and practical strategies, mentorship accelerates personal and professional growth. Whether it's refining communication, sharpening strategic thinking, or cultivating emotional intelligence, these skills form the foundation for confident and impactful leadership. Coaching and mentorship aren't just support systems – they are catalysts that enable women to master their craft and step boldly into their full potential.

THE LEADERSHIP EDGE: HOW COACHING AND MENTORING DRIVE SUCCESS

Access to coaches and mentors has consistently proven to be a transformative factor in empowering women to step confidently into leadership roles. By fostering a belief in their abilities, these relationships help women overcome doubts and embrace opportunities they may have once considered beyond their reach. Tanya, a successful executive, shared, *"Coaching and mentoring empowered me to take on leadership roles I initially felt unprepared for and achieve goals I once deemed unattainable."*

Mentorship also plays a critical role in reshaping perceptions of power. Mentors help women see themselves as capable and deserving leaders by demystifying leadership positions. Beyond confidence, coaching and mentorship equip women with essential leadership skills such as resilience, strategic planning, stress management, and the ability to recover from setbacks. These relationships also provide critical insights into navigating systemic barriers with clarity and determination.

Furthermore, mentees benefit from access to supportive networks and meaningful professional relationships that reinforce their confidence and expand their opportunities. Together, these elements create a powerful foundation for success, enabling women to rise into leadership roles with optimism, preparedness, and the belief that their impact can be significant and lasting.

NAVIGATING THE CHALLENGES: PITFALLS TO AVOID

- *Avoiding Overdependence*

While coaching and mentoring are invaluable tools for leadership growth, their effectiveness is deeply influenced by your circumstances and the social dynamics of your environment. To maximise the benefits, it is essential to create both an internal mindset and an external environment conducive to the success of these relationships.

One key consideration is to avoid overdependence on your coach or mentor. Coaching and mentorship are meant to empower you, not replace your agency. Always remember, you are the player on the field – they are there to guide you, not to play the game for you. The ultimate success of these relationships depends on your commitment to implementation. As the expert in your own life and career, you are responsible for identifying areas of growth, initiating action, and driving the outcomes you seek.

- *Long-Term Growth vs. Quick Fixes*

It's also important to use coaching and mentorship for long-term development rather than as a quick fix for urgent problems or damage control. Effective growth comes from a focus on sustainable strategies rather than immediate solutions.

- *Valuing Diverse Perspectives*

For women, the scarcity of female mentors due to historical under-representation in leadership roles means their time and guidance must be valued. While male mentors can be instrumental, it's important to recognise that they may not fully understand or relate to the unique challenges you face. A diverse mentoring network, therefore, can help you gain insights from multiple perspectives, enriching your growth and adaptability.

Coaching and mentorship are powerful catalysts for success when approached strategically. By taking ownership of your development and using these relationships to enhance your capabilities rather than relying on them as a crutch, you can truly unlock their potential to transform your leadership journey.

SUMMARY: OWNING YOUR GROWTH AND ELEVATING YOUR LEADERSHIP

Mastering the art of confidence through self-efficacy is not a luxury – it is your leadership imperative. As a woman, breaking barriers on the path to the boardroom, your belief in your capabilities must be consistently nurtured, guarded, and elevated.

This chapter has shown that coaching and mentorship are more than just professional development tools – they are transformational partnerships that shape your mindset, refine your skills, and solidify your confidence. They help you silence self-doubt, speak up with authority, and grow into the kind of leader others trust and follow.

But remember: The journey to the boardroom is yours to lead. Mentors and coaches can guide you, but only you can take the steps. When you combine self-efficacy with intentional growth, bold advocacy, and authentic leadership, you don't just belong in the boardroom – you command it. Now is the time to step into your power, elevate your voice, and lead with confidence. The seat at the table is already waiting for you.

CHAPTER 6
VISUALISE YOUR GOAL

"Without a vision, breaking into the boardroom remains a far-off dream."

From page one, my vision for *Breaking into the Boardroom* has been singular and clear: to get *you* into the boardroom. When I first conceived the idea for this book, I envisioned you – along with countless women around the world – successfully stepping into the boardroom, empowered and inspired by what you'd read. That vision is what brought these words from my heart and subconscious mind into your hands. That is the power of a clear vision – it becomes both the fuel and the compass for your aspirations.

As much as this has been my vision, it must now become yours. Take ownership of it. Remove all doubt. Believe, with everything in you, that you will make it into the boardroom.

VISION STARTS BY SEEING

Having vision starts with seeing it. You need to see yourself in the boardroom, leading, influencing, and effecting beneficial change in your organisation. Once you see the boardroom in your heart, you can see it with your eyes, because it becomes real to you. It becomes something you possess inside, regardless of your current job title or employee grade.

The inability to see a vision is the biggest hindrance that most people face in achieving their goals. This is because our minds don't naturally see what our eyes have not seen before. It is easier to create images in your heart of things that your eyes have seen before because it is familiar territory. That is why many people stay stuck in cycles of repeated failures and negative experiences, whether in their careers, health, or relationships.

We all know of someone who has lost and regained weight multiple times, or who has been divorced or dismissed from work more than once. It is not that these people intentionally set out to fail – it's because they have not seen a new vision of success in that particular area. Without a new vision, it's impossible to paint new mental pictures of victory.

You cannot live beyond the quality of the pictures you hold in your heart. Those inner pictures prepare you for success or set you up for failure. Now, let me show you some practical strategies to help you see your vision.

VISION-ENABLING TOOLS

1. Your Professional Vision Statement

Just as your company has a vision statement to guide its direction, you should also have a professional vision statement declaring your intention to occupy the boardroom. This is the first step to bringing your vision to life because it helps train your eyes to see what you desire in your heart. You become like an architect, who brings to life the full picture of what a property developer desires. Just as a building can't be constructed without a plan, your journey to success needs a clear picture of your destination.

Once you've crafted this vision statement, your goal becomes clearer and easier to work towards. It becomes something you can start building step by step, with purpose and strategy. Let's walk through how to draft your own professional vision statement.

ELEMENTS OF A WINNING PROFESSIONAL VISION STATEMENT

- *Aspirational and Inspirational*

Your professional vision statement captures the future that you want to see for your career. It should emphatically state the C-suite position that you want to occupy. As such, it has to be aspirational, indicating what you are striving for, as well as inspirational, evoking the desire to work towards its attainment.

- *Purpose-Oriented*

Indicate the "why" behind your desire to occupy the boardroom and the impact that your success is going to have on your organisation and its stakeholders. A strong "why" is the anchor of any vision; without one, your efforts can become unsustainable. This is why it is important for you to take some time to think about the areas of your career that you truly want to influence. These should be areas of real significance that will allow you to make a lasting impact.

- *Values-Centric*

Identify the principles that will always guide you in the execution of your tasks and interactions with others. These can include integrity, fairness, excellence, collaboration, continuous learning, and respect. Your values act as your moral compass, enabling you to act ethically at all times, preventing you from sacrificing your authentic self, and betraying the beliefs that you hold dear.

- *Short and Simple*

Keep your vision statement as clear and direct as possible so that anyone can understand it and connect to your vision. Simplicity is often underrated, but it's powerful because it removes unnecessary complexity and allows you to repeat and reinforce your vision regularly. When paired with clarity and brevity, simplicity helps you stay focused and keep your vision top of mind.

- *Practical and Focused*

Your statement should serve as a blueprint containing practical steps to turn your vision into a reality. Without actionable steps, your vision is confined to theory – it remains an idea, rather than a plan. In addition to practicality, your statement should reflect one vision. As the popular saying goes, "If you want to kill a man's vision, give him two." The same applies to us as women. Including too many aspirations in your vision statement will water it down and diminish its potency. Anyone who reads it, including you, should know that breaking into the boardroom is your top professional goal.

CRAFTING YOUR PROFESSIONAL VISION STATEMENT

Drafting your professional vision statement means incorporating all the elements that we have discussed so far – your "why", your values, simplicity, clarity, focus, and practical steps. It's not often that you see a professional vision statement in the public domain, so let's take a well-known company's vision statement and adapt it into something personal and aspirational. According to its website, Coca-Cola's vision statement reads as follows:

> *"Our vision is to craft the brands and choice of drinks that people love, to refresh them in body and spirit. And done in ways that create a more sustainable business and better future that makes a difference in people's lives, communities, and our planet."*

By deconstructing this vision statement, we can identify its structure. The first element is the main aspiration – crafting drinks that bring refreshment and joy. This is followed by a core value – sustainability. The third element is highlighting the intended impact – improving people's lives, their communities, and the planet. Lastly, it also refers to the future, indicating the long-term focus of the company's vision. These four elements make up the structure of the Coca-Cola company's vision statement.

Although short, the statement is inspirational because it talks of a vision that goes beyond producing beverages – it's about making a meaningful difference. In the same way, your professional vision statement should be short, clear, and driven by purpose.

Using these four elements in aspirational and inspirational language, write your professional vision statement in under five sentences For example, an aspiring CFO might say:

"My vision is to be the best Chief Financial Officer serving the Namibian banking sector. Through integrity, innovation, dedication, and collaboration, I will strive to create lasting value for my organisation and stakeholders whilst being an example and sponsor to the next generation of female leaders who aspire to follow in my footsteps."

Once you have drafted your unique professional vision statement, treat it with the same importance as your company's vision. Display it on your vision board and any other place where you'll see it often, such as the screensaver of your laptop or phone. Not only will this serve as a constant reminder of where your career is headed, but it will also help your subconscious mind to start forming a clear picture of you in the boardroom – confident, capable, and right where you belong.

2. Speak Your Vision

Seeing your vision statement is powerful - but speaking it out loud is even more impactful. When you vocalise your vision, your subconscious mind can hear the words contained in it. The dual impact of this audio and visual communication on your subconscious mind creates a vivid picture that strengthens your resolve. That is the reason why your words are so powerful. Once your subconscious mind hears them, it begins to build images based on the words you choose. As we discussed earlier, the quality of your images is determined by the type of words that you speak. Negative words produce limiting pictures that hold you back, whilst positive words create powerful, uplifting images.

Consider the countless stories of people who remember the significant impact of negative words spoken to them decades earlier by parents, teachers, and others in society. Some may proudly share how they achieved success despite hearing these words in their childhood. The mere fact that an adult can recall the impact of those negative words is proof that words are indeed powerful and can be scarring. Words have the power to shape futures.

Conversely, others fail to break out of the prison created by those negative words. They experience adulthood bound by fears and other self-sabotaging behaviours, which are a direct result of the pictures of unworthiness their subconscious minds would have painted, based on those words.

The difference between those who succeed and those who don't often comes down to the words they believe. The successful ones hear positive words, internalise them, and allow their subconscious minds to create new, empowering images. These new mental pictures replace the old ones of failure and become the foundation for lasting success. By speaking your vision aloud, you reinforce these positive images, aligning your heart and mind with your ultimate goals.

- *Automated For Success*

The main reason that seeing your vision with your heart automates you for success is because it makes your vision an internal reality. As mentioned earlier, once you can see the boardroom with the eyes of your imagination, it becomes real to you – even before it happens in the physical world. You begin to own the boardroom internally, regardless of your current job title or position.

Once your vision becomes part of your internal world, your subconscious mind starts directing all your energy, emotion, and effort towards bringing it to life. You'll begin to notice ideas and conversations that align with your goal as your mind alerts you to opportunities that you can take advantage of to achieve this end.

Let's prove this together. Think about a time you put a picture of a car that you wanted on your vision board. Suddenly, you started seeing the car, in the exact colour that you wanted, everywhere you went. It's not that these cars were previously hidden – they were always there, but your mind did not recognise them as important, therefore it allowed them to pass by without you noticing. This changed when you put the car onto your vision board. Your subconscious mind started alerting you each time you came in contact with the vehicle because it was highlighting any opportunity for you to acquire the car and bring your vision to life.

So, it is the same with your vision to break into the boardroom. Your subconscious mind will send you opportunity alerts. These are often referred to as hunches, and they will be littered along your journey to the boardroom. The key is to follow them and take advantage of them.

ADVANTAGES OF A PROFESSIONAL VISION STATEMENT

In addition to automating you for success, your professional vision statement helps you in various other ways as you work your way into the boardroom. We have already touched on some of them when we looked at the key elements of your professional vision statement. Let us expound on the notable ones and explore some of the others:

- *Clarity of Purpose and Direction*

By defining your career aims, your vision statement gives you a professional track on which to run throughout your career. This track is important because it provides a clear pathway towards the boardroom. It keeps your efforts directed towards achieving your goals by highlighting what is important and filtering out what is not. Anything that is outside of the track is a distraction that should be avoided at all costs.

Just like a compass, your vision will help you stay on course in times of uncertainty. When it comes to your journey to the boardroom, trust me when I say there will be many uncertain times. Along the way, you may encounter tempting opportunities that appear attractive but don't align with your long-term goals. Here, your vision statement will serve as a reminder of what matters to you the most, enabling you to stave off the distractions.

You will also be faced with difficulties that may make you want to give up – times when progress feels slow, or when the obstacles seem too big. In those moments, the strength of your "why" will be your anchor. It will remind you why you started, keep you grounded, and give you the courage and strength to push forward no matter the challenge.

- *Inspiration and Motivation*

Big vision statements motivate and inspire. They paint a compelling picture of your future, and every time you reflect on this image, a certain level of excitement should be triggered within you. This picture should invigorate you and make you feel like success is not just possible – it's inevitable. And when you believe that, you'll approach your journey with the confidence and drive of someone who knows they're going to win.

With this understanding, you can also use your vision statement as a yardstick of your inner state. If your vision ceases to excite you, this means one of two things. It might mean it was never the right vision for you, or there is an external factor that is causing you to be demotivated. Breaking into the boardroom is a high-stakes goal – and it can come with a lot of pressure. So, if you're feeling flat or overwhelmed, take time to prioritise your well-being and build in some self-care routines to safeguard your mental health.

- *Patience*

The long-term focus that your vision statement brings also helps to nurture patience. Every vision has its appointed time, which we unfortunately cannot control. Many people do not understand this, and they end up giving up on their visions.

Your vision may progress slowly, but this does not mean it isn't valid or achievable.

This is a powerful truth that I have learned over the years: the opportunity will come. Your job is to be ready when it does. What you need to work on is your preparation. Focus on growing your capacity to perform in the boardroom. Remember, when opportunity meets preparation, records are broken. But when opportunity meets unpreparedness, it can lead to disappointment or even embarrassment. So stay the course, do the work, and be ready for your moment.

- *Buy-In of Key Stakeholders*

A well-drafted, easy-to-understand vision also helps you rally the support you need. You are not an island – you need the buy-in from key individuals. If you are married with kids, your family must understand the level of commitment that is required of you to break into the boardroom. This usually includes additional time at work, evening or weekend courses, networking events, and upskilling through further studies. Even if your support network looks different, those close to you need to understand what you are trying to achieve so that they can allow you the necessary room to do so.

Likewise, getting the best out of coaches, mentors, and sponsors requires them to understand your vision fully. Your professional vision statement will show them this picture clearly, ensuring everyone is aligned and working towards the same goal.

A WINNING GAME PLAN

Once your professional vision statement is in place, you can map out a *game plan* that will enable you to step into the boardroom. This includes not only executing your strategy but also promoting yourself through fostering meaningful relationships. Breaking into the boardroom requires a **three-pronged approach**: demonstrating technical ability by delivering tangible results for your company, showcasing leadership by cultivating strategic relationships, and enhancing your soft skills.

1. Enhance Your Technical Abilities

In today's rapidly evolving business world, the key to consistently producing results lies in a commitment to continuous learning. As a leader, resolve to be someone who is always upskilling and staying ahead of industry trends. With technological advancements disrupting industries at an unprecedented pace, what works today may be outdated tomorrow. To remain relevant and impactful, leaders must adapt by learning, unlearning, and relearning as the environment demands.

I firmly believe that the illiterate of the 21st century is not someone who cannot read or write, but someone who refuses to embrace change and growth. This mindset creates an opportunity for forward-thinking leaders to become solution centres during times of transformation, positioning themselves as indispensable assets. By embracing continuous learning, leaders not only enhance their technical expertise but also increase their value to the company and readiness for boardroom opportunities.

Remember, you are never too qualified to learn something new in life. Every stage of your journey presents fresh opportunities to expand your knowledge and refine your skills. The question remains: Will you be one of those leaders who rise to the challenge, embrace the future, and lead with adaptability?

The path to the boardroom is paved for those who are willing to invest in their growth and stay ahead of the curve.

- *Deliver Results*

As a leader, the responsibility for outcomes ultimately rests on your shoulders. It is essential to step in and deliver results when no one else on your team can. Building a proven track record of delivering results not only inspires confidence in your subordinates but also earns the trust of your superiors. They need to believe they are entrusting leadership to someone capable of safeguarding the company's fortunes and driving its success to the next level. Results earn you respect throughout the organisation.

When I was tasked with establishing the Namibian Financial Intelligence Centre in 2006/7 as the project leader, it was a challenge unlike anything I had faced before. The responsibility of setting up a pivotal institution from scratch meant I had to take complete ownership of the project. I dedicated countless hours to navigating uncharted territory and went the extra mile to ensure the initiative's success. This unwavering commitment to delivering results not only earned me the respect of my peers but also the recognition of my superiors. It was a turning point in my career that opened doors I had never even dreamed of walking through.

It is evident that delivering results creates a lasting impact and sets the foundation for advancing your career. It's not just about meeting expectations – it's about exceeding them and building a legacy of excellence.

To distinguish yourself from the crowd and fast-track your promotion, there are moments when you need to "deliver a whale." This means taking bold, calculated risks to secure a prized client or provide a game-changing solution for your organisation. Candice's journey exemplifies this approach. Reflecting on her success, she shared, *"Driven by my ambition to make an impact at a national level, and then potentially cross-border at a continental and international level, I took on challenges and calculated risks."* By tackling challenges others avoided and putting her reputation on the line, Candice not only made a significant impact but also secured her promotion to an executive role.

Like Candice, you can identify areas where you can make the most impact in your organisation today. The biggest opportunities for advancement often lie behind the biggest challenges your organisation is facing. By solving these critical problems, you position yourself as an indispensable leader – taking significant steps towards the boardroom.

2. Foster Strategic Relationships

In corporate life, relationships are invaluable – you simply cannot put a price on them. As we've established, it's crucial to build rapport not only with those who rank below you but also with those above you. Doing so significantly increases your chances of securing a sponsor within the senior leadership of your organisation.

- *Attract Sponsors*

Unlike a mentor or coach, a sponsor doesn't provide career guidance or skills support. Instead, a sponsor uses their influence to open doors of opportunity for you. Importantly, like mentors, sponsors are not pursued – they are attracted. You attract a sponsor by positioning yourself as a worthy protégé: someone who is loyal, eager to learn and grow, and consistently delivers results for the organisation.

A sponsor is willing to put their reputation on the line by vouching for you and granting you access to their network, making it essential for you to value and nurture this relationship. Every organisation has senior leaders invested in developing future leaders. To get on their radar, focus on contributing to the success of your company with dedication and excellence.

3. Enhance Your Soft Skills

Soft skills are the cornerstone of effective leadership and are crucial for those aspiring to advance professionally. This area is often overlooked. While technical expertise may get you noticed, it's your ability to communicate, collaborate, and inspire others that earns you a seat at the table.

Leaders with strong soft skills can navigate complex interpersonal dynamics, build trust, and foster a culture of inclusivity and innovation. They also tend to attract sponsors and mentors more easily. In today's business landscape, emotional intelligence, adaptability, and strategic relationship-building are particularly vital, where success often depends on leading diverse teams and influencing stakeholders.

To enhance your soft skills, consider tools such as leadership coaching, emotional intelligence training, public speaking workshops, and mentorship programmes. As a coach, these are the areas of development that keep me busy most of the time – working with individuals to develop their soft skills.

Regular feedback from peers and mentors can also help you identify areas for growth. Additionally, practising active listening, engaging in team-building exercises, and utilising online platforms offering skill-building courses can significantly elevate your interpersonal effectiveness. Developing these skills is not just an advantage – it is a necessity for boardroom success.

BONUS TIP: REVERSE ENGINEERING THE SUCCESS OF OTHERS

In addition to delivering results, fostering strategic relationships, and enhancing your soft skills, another powerful strategy for advancing your career is reverse engineering the success of others. Identify individuals who have reached the positions you aspire to, and then study their journeys and look for lessons you can apply and build upon in your own career. Learning from others is easier than you might think – all it takes is the courage to reach out. Most people enjoy sharing their stories and accomplishments, as it's human nature to take pride in our achievements.

If direct access to these individuals isn't possible, leverage public resources. LinkedIn, for example, provides detailed profiles of many executives, showcasing their qualifications, career paths, and, in some cases, personal insights through articles and posts. Such platforms also offer an excellent opportunity to establish connections and initiate meaningful conversations. By studying and connecting with successful professionals, you can gain valuable insights and strategies to refine your path to success.

SUMMARY: LET YOUR VISION BE BOLD AND UNWAVERING

Breaking into the boardroom begins long before you step through its doors – it starts with a clear vision. When you see yourself there, speak it, and write it down, you begin to align every part of your being towards that reality. Your professional vision statement becomes your compass, guiding you with clarity, purpose, and conviction.

But vision alone is not enough. It must be backed by action – a winning game plan that includes delivering results, cultivating strategic relationships, and sharpening your soft skills. By embracing continuous growth and learning from those who've gone ahead, you position yourself not only to enter the boardroom but to lead with excellence once you're there.

Let your vision be bold. Let it be unwavering. And let it lead you to the top.

CHAPTER 7
POSITION YOURSELF FOR PROMOTION

"The call for promotion is constantly going out – stand out and step up."

Not only do I want you to say these words above – I want you to believe them. Because they are true. As an executive and transformational coach, far too often, I hear a bright but disillusioned career woman say, "Estelle, I love my job and the company I work for, but I am not seeing any prospects for growth. Opportunities for promotions are simply not coming my way." Sound familiar? Maybe you've heard someone else say something similar, or maybe you've felt that way yourself. If that's the case, I want to show you how you can experience a completely different reality in which you become a promotion magnet. In the next section, I'll share practical strategies that will give you the keys to unlock the doors of advancement in your career.

KEY 1 – THINK PROMOTION

- *Adopt the Mindset of Advancement*

Just like your vision, the first step to promotion is *seeing* it, and you cannot see it unless you *think* it. Thinking promotion entails developing a mindset that believes your morning affirmation unreservedly.

> *"Opportunities for promotion are abundant – and they're chasing me today."*

The reason I keep on saying that promotion opportunities are abundant is because I believe it. This belief is not based on wishful thinking but on the fact that there is an unending demand for great leaders in all organisations, including corporates. As long as sustainability, profitability, and growth are on the agenda, this demand will never go away, and your company is no exception.

Over the years, I have had the privilege of serving as an executive and non-executive board member in some of Namibia's biggest companies. One thing has remained true: finding great leaders has always been a top priority for these institutions. From team leads to department heads to the shareholders themselves, everyone is looking for great leaders.

Even in my business journey – as an entrepreneur owning multiple Kauai quick food outlets to now running my executive coaching practice, finding great leaders was and still is a necessity. So, if everyone in a position of responsibility is looking for someone to share that responsibility with, how can there be a lack of promotion opportunities for you? Right now, your team leader is looking for someone dependable to take on more, and it's time for you to stand out and be that team player they can rely on. That's the core of promotion: being entrusted with additional responsibility.

Now, some people might say, "Wait a minute Estelle, what about the pay increase or the job title change?" My answer? Stop approaching your career with a purely transactional mindset. Yes, pay increases and new job titles are sometimes by-products of additional responsibilities, but the real prize is being entrusted with those additional responsibilities. Do not get me wrong, I am not saying pay increases and job title changes are not important – I celebrated each one I received, as they not only increased my financial status but boosted my confidence and job satisfaction. However, what I found was that as I diligently executed my additional responsibilities, the pay increases and title changes followed naturally. So shift your focus. Seek to be entrusted. That's where the real opportunity lies – and you'll soon realise there's no shortage of doors waiting to open for you.

KEY 2 – DEVELOP A PROMOTION-ATTRACTING CHARACTER

The reason why the second part of your daily affirmation says opportunities for promotion are chasing you is because you can develop your character into one that naturally attracts promotion. The most important hinge on which the doors to promotion will swing is your character. Trust me when I say that you cannot rise and stay at a level that your character isn't equipped to handle.

Your dream to break into the boardroom will stand or fall based on the strength of your character. Despite being technically gifted, I have seen many promising professionals fail to make it into leadership because of various character flaws. These individuals fail to realise that it's not just being great at your own job that gets you into leadership, but rather it is the positive influence you wield within the circle of your team members.

So, as you work towards your next promotion, consider how you are going to enhance your character to grow your influence amongst your current team members. To help you do this, let's explore some essentials that shape a character capable of attracting leadership opportunities. These are based on personal observation. Feel free to add to this list as you reflect on your own experiences on your journey to the boardroom.

- *Be Faithful to Build Trust*

Being found faithful is a non-negotiable for anyone who aspires to be promoted. This is because promotion flows in the direction of faithfulness. You may be wondering what faithfulness in the workplace looks like and how it relates to promotion. To give context and make the connection clearer, let us do a quick exercise. Think about the word *faithful*. Now write down another word that stands out to you the most when you hear that word. Take a minute and really reflect. What word have you written down? I have written down *loyal*. In my view, loyalty lies at the core of faithfulness – it's the foundation. So let us explore what this means in a professional setting.

- *Commit to the Vision*

Faithful people are committed people – and in the workplace, committed people are those who are totally aligned with the vision of their team leads. In a corporate setting, every employee – no matter their title – is a part of a team. If you are a sales agent, you are a part of the sales team. If you are the sales manager, you are a part of the management team. Even executives, including the Chief Executive Officer, belong to the executive team.

Each team works together to champion the broader vision of the organisation. And, within each team is a team lead who drives its mandate, as trickled down from those higher up in the organisation. Your employer trusts this team lead to deliver results, and if the team fails, it's the team lead who's ultimately held accountable.

Because of that responsibility, your team lead will usually develop a vision for the team – one that supports the overall direction of the company. As the custodian, your team lead then communicates this vision to their team, you included, expecting support and cooperation.

Let me re-emphasise this: as a faithful team player, harbouring dreams of breaking into the boardroom via promotion, you need to fully commit to the vision of your team lead. Promotion really can be that simple. Help your team leader achieve their goals, and you will naturally position yourself to be promoted. Trust me, this works time and time again.

- *Stay Loyal Under Pressure*

At this point, you might be saying, "Estelle, you do not know who my team lead is. They are so unfair – I will never get a promotion." We're going to discuss this issue of the relationship with your team lead shortly, but before we get there, let me assure you of this: even if your current team lead is holding back, your leadership capacity will speak for itself. You'll become so promotion-ready that someone else in a position of influence will notice. Whether it's within your current organisation or elsewhere, your value will shine through.

Faithful, committed professionals are hard to ignore – you may be headhunted, or your CV may become too good to pass up simply because of the impact you've consistently made in your present team.

- *Handle Offence with Maturity*

Before we discuss the other traits of loyalty, let's address the issue of dealing with difficult team leads. This is a pivotal matter, as it often derails many from being loyal to the vision of their team leaders. A person who feels unfairly treated by a particular individual is less likely to be invested in that person's success – that would be anyone's default response. Unfortunately, having that attitude towards your team lead means that you are disinvesting in your own success and resulting promotion as well.

With my experience in both corporate and leadership coaching spaces, I can confidently say that not all team leads are easy to work with. Some may be demanding, uncommunicative, or even difficult to engage. Others may be downright toxic. Let me be clear – staying in a toxic or abusive work environment is never a prerequisite for promotion, nor should it ever be.

As a woman on a mission to break into the boardroom, your well-being and professional integrity must remain a priority. Abuse, harassment, discrimination, and intimidation are never acceptable, and you should never have to "endure" them for the sake of career progression. In such cases, you have every right to raise your voice, protect your boundaries, seek support, and if necessary, walk away with your dignity intact.

However, there are also times when the challenge is not abuse, but friction or disappointment in your current leader. In those cases, growth is possible – and in fact, it is powerful. The truth is, promotion does not always come from your direct leader. It can come through your visible leadership impact, your consistency, your resilience, and the influence you build across the organisation. When your value is undeniable, someone will notice – if not in your current team, then in another one.

This is where emotional maturity comes in. Learn to separate the *person* from the *purpose*. If your leader is difficult but not abusive, choose to grow through the discomfort. Develop the emotional fortitude to keep showing up with excellence, even when you feel unseen or undervalued. Why? Because your standard is not about them – it's about you. It's about your leadership DNA and the woman you are becoming.

There is an African proverb that says, *"The axe forgets, but the tree never forgets."* Those who make our work lives difficult may be oblivious to the effects of their behaviour, while we carry the weight of those experiences for far too long. But if the individual who acted insensitively has already moved on without a second thought, why should you continue to carry the burden of resentment? Toughening up isn't about excusing harmful behaviour; it's about freeing yourself from the unhelpful emotions that keep you from focusing on your own growth.

Let go, refocus, and carry on. The boardroom requires a woman who can lead herself before leading others. And that includes knowing when to brush off others' negative behaviour and keep rising.

- *Avoid the Trap of Bitterness*

Do not allow negative people to occupy space in your mind and rob you of your energy. This is the space and energy that you need to freely express your brilliance in your career and advance to the boardroom. So, find a way to put the drama into perspective and work on having a functional relationship with your team leader.

Developing a thick skin prevents you from being easily offended. Interestingly, the Greek word for offence is *skandalon*, which refers to a bait, trap, or stumbling block. In the context of your career, the purpose of this trap is to derail you from the path to the boardroom. So you take this bait when you decide to quit your job or to become disloyal to your team leader's vision because you feel offended.

It is important to recognise that it is not only your team leader who can offend you. Your fellow team members, other colleagues, customers, work pressures, or anything else that makes you think of quitting can be a source of offence. Your team members can turn against you, gossip behind your back, or even spread lies about you. There may even be times when you feel you are being treated unfairly by being overlooked for promotion, for instance. This trap can come from anywhere. The trap of offence can come from many directions, but what keeps you on track is refusing to take the bait every time it's offered.

A thick skin will help you to remain focused on the goal, taking hurt and disappointment in your stride and soldiering on. It also helps you to avoid assuming that every negative experience is a personal attack. It's worth noting here that having an inflated ego can make it especially difficult not to take offence. When your sense of self is tied too tightly to how others treat you, even small slights can feel deeply personal.

- *Embrace Humility*

Humility is essential on your journey to the boardroom. It means you do not overestimate yourself. You do not think of yourself more highly than you should, as someone who is beyond the hurts and disappointments caused by others. But it also does not mean underestimating yourself or allowing others to walk all over you.

True humility comes from a self-awareness of your value. It allows you to handle offence with perspective, building your resilience, and helping you keep moving forward. So even when you are insulted or undermined, humble yourself, remain cool, and keep your eyes on the prize, which is the boardroom.

- *Serve Your Team*

Serving is the hallmark of loyalty. Being fully committed to the vision of your team leader means supporting your entire team. This involves assisting everyone in your team to achieve their goals. You become a helping hand and a problem solver. I know it sounds like a tall order, but this is how you attract influence and become deserving of promotion. When you serve others, you show them that you care about them, and as Theodore Roosevelt said, *"People don't care how much you know until they know how much you care."* When your team knows how much you care, they start to value your knowledge, and your influence grows. In essence, by developing a heart of service towards your team, you automatically position yourself as a leader within the group. This is the simplest and most effective promotion hack: if you are seen as a leader before you are officially promoted, such a promotion is easy because it becomes a mere formality.

- *Be Dependable*

As you endeavour to serve your team to the best of your abilities, ensure that you maintain a high degree of dependability. This is because trust grows influence. Your team leader should be able to rely on you to complete the tasks they assign to you.

Furthermore, whoever you agree to help in your team should know that you deliver on your commitments. Be a person of your word, keeping your promises and maintaining trust and confidence.

- *Keep Healthy Boundaries*

While having a heart of service involves being available to help others, maintaining trust also requires you to say "no" when you are unable to offer any assistance. Setting clear boundaries builds trust – not only with others, but with yourself. Boundaries define what's acceptable and what's not, what's available and what's off limits. A simple, respectful "no" or "I can't" – even without explanation – maintains more trust and integrity than an unfulfilled promise.

The inability to say "no" is a common problem for many people across the world. This is mainly due to cultural influences or individual shortcomings. So if you struggle to say "no", the good news is that your problem is not unique – and there are readily available solutions for you.

The first point of call would be to take some time for personal introspection to understand why this is the case. Is it that you genuinely want to always be available to assist others, or is it that you fear some sort of backlash that may result from disappointing them?

First of all, the fact remains: your capacity to assist is limited because you are just one person and you have multiple professional and personal responsibilities. As such, you simply can't be available to help others all the time.

Secondly, the fear of reprisal is more of a problem on your end than on the person you will be saying no to. It often stems from an unhealthy need for acceptance and popularity, which leads to a people-pleaser mindset. Unfortunately, this mindset works against your efforts to grow influence within your team. Instead of attracting influence, it repels it. The value of your efforts in your team's eyes diminishes once they realise that they are not based on a genuine desire to help, but on a need for approval or acceptance. They may no longer believe that you truly care about them – as a result, your voice could lose its importance.

If you believe that you have been struggling with this fear of rejection, I encourage you to confront it head-on. First of all, the potential backlash you fear of being rejected by team members because you are not able to assist is exaggerated and false. Ask yourself – when was the last time you rejected someone because they genuinely could not assist you? It has never happened, right?

Secondly, your worth as a person is not based on what you do for others It is rooted in the simple fact that you are part of this amazing human race, just like everyone else. So if anyone rejects you because of an unfounded reason, that is their problem, not yours.

- *Commit to the Long Haul*

The journey to the boardroom is long and, as we have established earlier, fraught with many challenges, hurts, and disappointments. To remain loyal through it all, you need patience. It is the anchor that keeps you faithful in the face of adversity. Attracting promotion requires making a long-term commitment to breaking into the boardroom. As we discovered in Chapter 6, we do not have control over when promotion comes, but we do have control over our actions in pursuit of it. That means our commitment to the boardroom must last until the mission is accomplished – however long that takes.

Patience enables you to endure the uncertainty and frustration that may come with this open-ended journey. It helps you stay the course and allows you to get to the finish line. Patience works hand in hand with humility and sustains your thick skin, making you more resilient to the challenges that come your way.

- *Establish Strong Roots*

In addition to helping you stay loyal, one of the great benefits of patience is that it allows you to develop the root system that you need to sustain promotion. Consider how the Chinese bamboo tree grows. It's said that this plant takes up to five years to break through the ground and emerge as a sprout. For five whole years after the seed has been planted, there is no visible growth above the surface. Imagine being the person caring for this tree – watering it, fertilising it, and carefully nurturing it – but having nothing to show for your effort. Most of us would be discouraged and probably quit.

But in the fifth year, however, seemingly out of nowhere, the plant shoots up a staggering 80 to 90 feet within the first six weeks. It becomes one of the fastest-growing trees in the world. So what supports that sudden surge of growth when nothing seemed to be happening during those early years? On the contrary, something was happening. The tree was developing a strong underground root system robust enough to support and sustain this phenomenal growth. In the same way, patience helps you develop the necessary capacity needed to carry the added responsibilities that come with promotion.

- *Stay Open to Learning*

Another essential character trait that attracts influence and promotion is teachability. For you to function effectively in a team and grow your influence, you need to have a teachable spirit. This means that you are open to learning as well as implementing new ideas. It means that you are humble enough to accept that you do not know everything and that your ways of doing things may not always be the best.

In this fast-paced, technology-driven business world, dynamics are constantly changing. On the one hand, team members are expected to collaborate to bring solutions, and effective collaboration is only possible when team members are open to learning from one another. On the other hand, team leaders value teachable individuals who are quick to grasp new instructions and adapt to new strategies. If you want to grow your influence with your team leader, become proficient at following their lead.

Again, I have seen gifted professionals miss out on advancement simply because of an unwillingness to follow the guidance of the team leaders. In today's world, where information is readily available, some may believe the illusion that access to knowledge makes them experts. However, no matter how much you know, if you want to advance in a corporate environment, following the direction of your leaders is non-negotiable.

Every team leader has their own way of operating, and it is your duty as a team member to conform. Remember, your team lead is the custodian of the team's vision. If the team fails to meet its goals, the responsibility falls on the lead. However, if the failure occurs due to a lack of unity in execution, it becomes the fault of those who refused to be teachable.

Following your team leader's direction has the additional benefit of protecting you from unconscious incompetence. When you lack experience in a certain area, you have the unfortunate privilege of not knowing what you do not know. This means you are not aware of the deficiencies in your understanding because you are not familiar with the subject. For an unteachable person, such a scenario often ends in disaster, as overconfidence combined with a lack of knowledge will likely result in mistakes.

In contrast, a teachable person, by listening to instruction, gains experience and familiarity with the subject and recognises their lack of knowledge and skill. At this point, they become consciously incompetent, which drives them to work at acquiring the relevant skill and knowledge to move into competence.

KEY 3 – DEVELOP CHEMISTRY AND CONNECTION

Without chemistry or connection, no two people – let alone a team – can work productively together. Growing influence with your team members means developing professional chemistry with them. Granted, personalities may be different, but there should be some form of mutual understanding that binds people together to work collaboratively and harmoniously. As someone who is seeking promotion, your goal should be to assist your team lead with developing team chemistry. So firstly, you have to avoid acting in ways that are detrimental to the unity of the team, and secondly, you have to actively cultivate strong relationships.

The bedrock of chemistry in any team is trust. Each member has to know that their teammates have their back and this is done by cultivating and encouraging selflessness in the team.

- *Promote Shared Goals*

The promotion of shared goals brings about unity of purpose. Instead of each team member existing and working in silos, the effort must be organised so that everyone works towards the team's greater goal. It is just like in a soccer match, a striker cannot only be concerned with scoring goals – at some point, they have to fall back and defend their team's goal. For this level of collaboration to succeed, there needs to be effective communication. Each party must clearly understand the other's expectations.

- *Cultivate Connection Within Professional Boundaries*

Although the emphasis is on maintaining professional relationships, there should also be opportunities to build personal connections, where team members get to know each other through informal team outings such as lunches and team-building activities. This fosters a sense of mutual care for each other in a safe, team-driven environment.

KEY 4 – LEARN THE UNSPOKEN LANGUAGE OF CULTURE

The culture of an organisation is often defined as the collection of values, beliefs, ethics, and attitudes that characterise its people and guide their practices. It forms the basis of a company's essence or DNA distinguishing it from other organisations. When you hear a company's employee say, "That's just the way we do things around here," they are referring to the company's culture. It is an intangible thread that holds a company together, which is why every successful organisation places such a strong emphasis on it.

Renowned management consultant Peter Drucker is often credited with the quote, "Culture eats strategy for breakfast." This means no matter how great a company's business strategy is, it will fail without a strong culture to support it.

Successful companies realise this and they guard their cultures jealously – and they don't promote anyone who does not embody it.

- *Assess Cultural Alignment*

As a leader, your job is to promote and reinforce company culture within the organisation. But that's an impossible task if you do not embrace the company culture yourself. If you're aiming for promotion, it's essential that you know and understand your company's culture inside and out. If not, please take the time to do so.

This will help you assess whether you are aligned with what your company represents – especially if you're hoping to contribute at the highest level: the boardroom. If you are not aligned, it may be worth considering whether a different organisation, one that shares your values and outlook, might be a better fit. After all, the work you do every day should be in harmony with your true self.

SUMMARY: RISE, READY, AND RECOGNISED

Promotion is not a stroke of luck – it is the natural reward for a deliberate mindset, a refined character, and a consistent display of leadership potential. There is no shortage of opportunities; there is only a shortage of those prepared to seize them.

When you think about promotion, live faithfully, develop influence, stay teachable, build team chemistry, and embody company culture, you position yourself as an undeniable force for growth within any organisation.

So, stand out. Be counted. And when the call for promotion goes out – let it find you ready. The boardroom is not beyond you, it is awaiting you.

CHAPTER 8
ADDRESSING WORK-LIFE IMBALANCES

"The boardroom is one chapter of your life's story: It is not the entire book."

One of the biggest challenges that I have faced throughout my professional career is finding the right work–life balance. From the first day that I set foot in corporate Namibia, my goal was to give myself wholly to my work. I applied myself diligently, put in the hours, and continuously upskilled myself through further studies. This approach paid dividends quickly, as I managed to break into my first boardroom in my early thirties, a feat that I am still proud of today.

My career was progressing well, but I was fortunate enough to realise early on that work was only one part of my life and not my entire life. Outside of work, other aspects of my life required a similar level of success, if not more. I was a young wife and mother. My husband needed a great and supportive spouse, and my children needed me to be a loving and present parent. My parents and siblings also needed me to play an active role in their lives. Not only that, but I also had to nourish my spirit, body, and soul, because everything else I was building rested on that foundation.

When I transitioned into entrepreneurship and became my *own boss*, the need to maintain this balance was heightened. Without prior industry experience, I acquired and ran the Kauai Namibia master franchise successfully for several years. If you have ever built a business, you'll understand the amount of effort and sacrifice this requires.

After exiting the franchise, I established E-merge Coaching in February 2021. Since then, I have spent an enormous amount of time away from home, travelling throughout the country and regionally to empower various groups of clients. This, by the way, is only one part of the business. There's also the core work of Executive and Transformational Coaching, plus the authoring of books and other written resources.

Alongside all of this, I've remained committed to continuous learning and upskilling. This resulted in the proud milestone of graduating with merit in November 2024, with an MBA in Coaching, Mentoring, and Leadership.

While I've pursued excellence in my business career, the demands of my personal life haven't lessened – they've grown. My little girls became teenagers, requiring a whole advanced level of parenting skills. I'm proud to say I have been there every step of the way. A special highlight for me was recently escorting my eldest to South Africa as she enrolled for her first year of university.

I've shared all of the above not to blow my own horn, but to show you that it *is* possible to pursue excellence in your quest for the boardroom whilst still succeeding in all the other important roles in your life. This was a non-negotiable for me because I promised myself early on that I would not allow myself to be a public success and a private failure.

It's no good being celebrated at the office whilst your personal life is falling apart. A hero at work but a villain at home. Loved by strangers, but resented by those who should love you the most.

At this point, you might be saying, "Estelle, I hear you, but how am I going to play all the other roles in my life successfully *and* pursue the boardroom? There is only one of me, and in all honesty, I don't think I can do both."

I will be the first one to admit that getting this balancing act right is *not* easy. It is a dance I had to learn through trial and error, falling and getting up many times before mastering. But here is the most important lesson I learned along the way…

BALANCE STARTS FROM WITHIN

The key to achieving work–life balance is having *inner* balance. You cannot create balance on the outside if you don't have it within, because inner balance is the foundation of outer balance.

So, what is inner balance? It's your mental and emotional well-being. It allows you to successfully break into the boardroom *and* live a fulfilled life at the same time.

As societal and economic pressures continue to increase strain on employees, it is no secret that mental health has become a topical issue in workplaces across the world. In response to a fast-paced and constantly changing business environment, companies are increasingly expecting employees to do more with less. This work strain is exacerbated by the many pressures that employees face at home.

Life is not a bed of roses – everyone is going through something. This is an important realisation that I can relate to as I progressed into adulthood and gained more life experience. People can wear smiles on their faces while facing difficult life circumstances. From the outside, you'd never know that someone is going through a divorce, is suffering from some form of abuse, or is dealing with illness in a child, a parent, or even themselves.

Whereas the old work culture expected employees to suck it up, leave their problems at home, and deliver results, it has become evident that this is not possible. Employees carry the weight of their personal problems into the workplace, affecting their productivity and overall work experience. As women – often the most vulnerable in society – we are particularly susceptible to these home pressures. Coupled with the gender-based discrimination that many of us face, it comes as no surprise that workplace research has shown female employees to be more stressed than their male counterparts. For example, the 2024 *Deloitte Women @ Work: A Global Outlook* report surveyed 5000 women from workplaces across ten countries. Half of the respondents indicated feeling more stressed than they did in 2023 and expressed serious concern about their mental health. A staggering 23% (that's 1150 women) stated that they felt burnt out.

Burnout has become so prevalent in the workplace that it was included as an occupational phenomenon by the World Health Organization (WHO) in the 11th Revision of the International Classification of Diseases. While it stopped short of classifying it as a medical condition, the WHO defined burnout as a syndrome emanating from chronic workplace stress that has not been successfully managed.

Burnout typically shows up as mental, emotional, and physical exhaustion. It invokes feelings of inadequacy – a sense that you're not performing well in the workplace and that you're powerless to turn the situation around. This heightens anxiety levels and strips away any excitement about your current job and future career prospects.

In an effort to cope, some employees begin to mentally detach from their jobs, resulting in increased absenteeism. For others, unchecked burnout can unfortunately lead to more serious health conditions such as depression, high blood pressure, and heart disease.

Here we are referring to the ordinary female employee, so you can only imagine how much more vulnerable to stress a woman leader striving to break into the boardroom becomes. Sharing her perspective on this matter, Beverly stated,

> *"As I grow older and gain more experience, I find the challenges I face becoming increasingly daunting. Sometimes, I can't help but think it might have been easier if I were a man. However, being a woman also brings a unique perspective to the table. Balancing the responsibilities of motherhood, especially as a single parent, while also sitting at the executive table presents significant challenges. Unlike our male counterparts, we often don't have the luxury of someone at home managing these challenges, which adds an extra layer of complexity to our work–life balance as female leaders."*

Beverly's candid revelation highlights the unique challenges women face in their quest to achieve work–life balance, especially when they lack domestic support, as many do. By using the word *daunting* she also reveals how these challenges can trigger feelings of being overwhelmed and affect one's inner balance. If you relate to Beverly's experience, or if you find your mental and emotional well-being affected due to other circumstances, let me share some tools that can assist you in restoring your inner balance.

ACKNOWLEDGE THE PROBLEM

The first step to solving any problem is acknowledging it. I do not like being sick, but I have learned to be honest with myself when it comes to any issue concerning my health and wellness. This does not make me come across as weak, but rather it empowers me to be a good steward of my physical, mental, and emotional well-being. I know you have heard it countless times, but your health is truly your wealth. Without it, breaking into the boardroom whilst living a fulfilled life becomes far more difficult. When illness strikes, your health challenge takes centre stage in your life.

I once heard someone say, "Your many life problems quickly become one when you are confronted with a health challenge." If you've read my first book, *Breaking Barriers*, you'll know that I experienced the brutal truth of this statement back in 2012. An illness requiring a six-month recovery period stopped my successful corporate career at the Bank of Namibia dead in its tracks. I had to hand in my resignation, and just like that, the curtain was drawn on my illustrious 18-year career in Namibia's finance sector.

So, if you are not feeling well mentally or emotionally, be honest with yourself and acknowledge it. There is no shame in doing so. We are living in fast-paced, high-pressure times with many challenges. The internet has put the entire world at our fingertips, and we want to experience the best of what it has to offer. Professionally and personally, we are expected to continuously strive for the best, and the finish line keeps moving further and further away.

In addition, the same internet bombards us with a constant deluge of negative messaging. We are exposed to every global tragedy in real time, from plane crashes to wars to natural disasters caused by extreme weather events. We don't even have to wait for the evening news on TV or check the morning paper anymore – it's all right there on our phones, all the time. If left unchecked, this constant exposure to bad and often traumatic news can form a pessimistic mindset, harming our mental and emotional well-being.

TRACE THE SOURCE

Once you have acknowledged the problem, you can now trace its source to solve it. This is because problems are solved at the root and not the fruit. Once the problem at the root is dealt with, the fruit can flourish. In the previous section, we identified two factors that can disrupt inner balance: the constant pursuit of perfection and the never-ending exposure to the negative news of the world.

Before we explore additional factors, I want to re-emphasise the importance of dealing with unresolved trauma and silencing the noise as we discussed in earlier chapters. I believe this is the foundation of inner balance, and without it, all our efforts in this area become cosmetic. So, if you are still struggling with building this foundation, revisit those sections and identify any gaps you may have experienced implementing the provided solutions. In the meantime, let us look at some additional factors that can disrupt your inner balance.

- Failure to Disconnect from Work

Advancements in remote working technologies have revolutionised the way we work by eliminating most geographic and time limitations when it comes to service-based jobs. Gone are the days when work was confined to office buildings, landlines, and physical files. Now everything lives in the cloud and as long as you have your cell phone and laptop, you can be expected to put in some work anywhere.

There is no doubt that the ability to work remotely has given our generation a massive advantage over past generations by increasing our capacity to do much more in a 24-hour time frame. But on the downside, this blessing has, for many, become a curse by blurring the lines between work and our personal lives. Just under 2000 of the 5000 women participating in the 2024 Deloitte Report stated that they found it difficult to disconnect from work, whilst nearly 1000 indicated that they regularly worked overtime. That is close to 40% and 20% respectively – a clear sign that the pressure to always be in work mode is taking its toll.

To confirm that this failure to disconnect from work does indeed disrupt inner balance, only 23% of the women who regularly work overtime reported that their mental health was good. This was in contrast to the 50% of those who did *not* regularly work overtime, who said the same. As we can see, consistently working overtime and failing to disconnect from work makes one twice as vulnerable to inner imbalance compared to those who work regular hours.

In my experience, there are three main reasons why one would struggle to disconnect from work. Let us explore them below.

- *Overly Demanding Employers*

As mentioned earlier, as the global economy tightens and globalisation increases competition amongst corporates, more is being expected from employees. To some extent, this expectation is reasonable – everyone can be expected to roll up their sleeves when the going gets tough. However, it becomes unreasonable when the cost is the mental health and overall well-being of employees. At that point, employers need to assess the bottom line and invest in additional resources.

- *Ambition*

Unlike the scenario above, some employees fail to disconnect from work because of their own ambition. They buy into the so-called "hustle culture" prevalent in some corporate organisations and start-ups. This culture glorifies work success above all else. Those who put in the longest hours and take the least time off are celebrated, whilst those who stick to "normal" work hours and use their leave days are vilified or looked down upon.

With this hustle culture, it is not about just achieving your basic targets and meeting your KPIs. There is always more to achieve, a bigger deal, or a more prestigious promotion. With this mindset, doing the bare minimum isn't seen as an option. Believing this is the only key to advancement, some employees unfortunately adopt – and even promote – this unhealthy way of working.

As much as some advocates of this so-called hustle culture argue that it promotes innovation and growth, I doubt that it comes without disruption to one's inner balance. Known to work 50 – 60 hours per week, those immersed in this culture undoubtedly do so at the expense of adequate sleep, especially if one factors in other day-to-day life activities.

Studies conducted by the US Government Centers for Disease Control and Prevention (CDC) define inadequate sleep as getting six hours or less per night on average. They revealed that those who have inadequate sleep are 2.5 times more likely to suffer from mental distress than those who get enough rest. Inadequate sleep has also been linked to mood swings, increased irritability, and impatience, and in more serious cases, it can lead to conditions such as anxiety, depression, and paranoia.

Mentally exhausted employees are likely to make errors, struggle to complete tasks, and experience reduced creativity – all of which are counterproductive to the goal of the hustle culture, which is to achieve more success.

In addition to exposing one to the inner imbalance that comes with inadequate sleep, the psychology around hustle culture is also detrimental to one's mental and emotional well-being. Working in an environment with ever-increasing expectations and continuously increasing targets removes the positive effect that comes with a sense of accomplishment. Furthermore, striving to meet the unrealistic notion that there is always more to achieve, regardless of the true conditions affecting a business – such as market forces and resources – can leave employees disillusioned. Some may also adopt a sense of unwarranted guilt, as they blame themselves for not achieving expectations that were misplaced to begin with. Stress and anxiety over job security will undoubtedly come with the package.

- *Inefficiency in Execution*

Failing to complete tasks quickly and efficiently can lead to difficulties with disconnecting from work. Uncompleted work tends to linger in your mind even after clocking off. So even if you are not working physically, you maintain a mental connection with work, which prevents you from switching off and truly resting. Furthermore, constant thoughts of unfinished tasks can lead to feelings of being left behind and out of control. Your inner balance is disrupted as panic and anxiety set in. As this inefficiency continues, work piles up, making it more difficult to disconnect from work – and so the vicious cycle continues.

A TOXIC WORK ENVIRONMENT

One thing that we have established throughout this book is that the workplace can be a challenging place. That is the core premise of this book: overcoming challenges and breaking into the boardroom. As a career woman, it is unfortunately commonplace to face gender-based discrimination and various forms of microaggression. Although these acts can be hurtful and upsetting, causing mental and emotional distress, we have already established that you can develop a thick skin and thrive despite them.

So, when does a challenging environment cross the threshold into toxicity? In my view, this is when you are subjected to outright harassment or other forms of conduct that undermine your dignity and self-worth in the workplace. As we touched on in Chapter 7, this is conduct that is so intolerable, agonising, or unendurable that you cannot be expected to continue with your employment without it being resolved. Such conduct is deeply damaging to your mental and emotional well-being. It's far more than just upsetting – it can include physical and verbal bullying, intimidation, online or in-person harassment, as well as psychological abuse.

A LACK OF DOMESTIC SUPPORT

Our societies have long dictated that a woman's primary responsibility is the upkeep of her home and the welfare of those who live in it. This is a deeply entrenched legacy of patriarchy which is, in my view, almost inescapable. No matter how successful our careers become or how demanding our jobs are, we're expected to be homemakers. It is as if society says, "Yes, we allowed you to go into the workforce, but don't forget your husband and children at home."

It is not uncommon to hear comments like, "Amanda just got a big promotion at her company, but it's a pity that she doesn't have a husband or children to enjoy all that success with." This notion – that a woman cannot be complete without marriage or children can trigger feelings of inadequacy and become a significant source of emotional and mental distress. It ignores preferences and freedom of choice. Some women may not want to get married or have children. Additionally, it unfairly disregards the fact that women are not in full control of these outcomes. Traditionally, women are not the initiators of marriage, and many silently battle fertility challenges, which, in themselves, can be sources of great emotional and mental anguish.

During our interview, Dantagos shared a powerful insight concerning the connection between romantic relationship choices and career success for ambitious women. She said,

> *"Who you marry or are in a relationship with as a female leader matters, because then it's a function of whether your spouse can hold your greatness or the greatness that ought to come out of you. If you choose wrong, it can inhibit your growth."*

Wow, what a powerful statement. I could not have said it better myself. The people we choose to marry or enter into committed relationships with must be able to hold our greatness – or the greatness that is yet to emerge.

As a naïve young adult, I did not fully understand when I heard people say that marrying the wrong person is one of the worst decisions you could make. As I gained a bit more life experience, I began to see what these people meant. There are countless people in the world whose entire lives and careers were derailed by being in a marriage or romantic relationship with the wrong person. Without going into detail, we all know the mental and emotional anguish that can come from abusive or unhealthy relationships. This, of course, applies to both men and women, but because women are often more vulnerable, they tend to suffer more.

Assuming the relationship is healthy, the person you commit to must also be in a position to offer significant domestic support if you're going to successfully manage your home life whilst you pursue a career in the boardroom.

According to the 2024 Deloitte Report, this is unfortunately not the case for most women. Even when living with a partner – and even when earning more than them – women still carry the greater share of domestic responsibility. This includes childcare, caring for adults, domestic tasks such as cleaning, and home management activities such as shopping for household items and managing finances.

In terms of impact on inner balance, only 35% of these women reported that their mental health was good. This is significantly lower than the 47% of women whose partners either took the lead on these responsibilities or shared them equally.

Even more concerning is the link between a lack of support at home and the inability to disconnect from work. Among the women who carried the greatest domestic responsibility, only 32% found it easy to switch off – compared to 40% of those with supportive partners.

These numbers clearly show that a lack of domestic support is a double-edged sword, disrupting mental and emotional well-being and hindering the ambitions of women.

In the following chapter, we'll explore the solutions to the factors disrupting your inner balance and also look at further methods of enhancing your work–life balance.

SUMMARY: BALANCE IS YOUR BIRTHRIGHT

Finding balance is not about choosing between success and well-being – it's about designing a life where both coexist and thrive. You are not just a leader in the boardroom; you are a whole person with dreams, relationships, responsibilities, and a soul that needs nurturing.

As this chapter has shown, inner balance is the foundation for outer excellence. You *can* pursue greatness in your career without sacrificing your mental health, your peace, or your joy. But it starts with awareness, intentionality, and bold decisions that protect your well-being. The boardroom is just one chapter in your life's story – make sure the rest of the story is just as powerful, purposeful, and fulfilling.

CHAPTER 9
BALANCING AMBITION, WELLNESS, AND HOME

"Your professional success should never come at a cost so high that your personal life pays the price."

In the previous chapter, we pulled back the curtain on a hard truth: many women on the path to leadership are being stretched too thin. We are not just navigating boardrooms – we are carrying households, fighting invisible battles, and trying to find space for ourselves in between.

We named the real barriers: toxic work cultures, blurred boundaries between work and life, the constant pressure to over-perform, and the societal expectation that women must succeed professionally without ever letting their domestic responsibilities slip. We acknowledged that burnout is no longer a rare condition but a growing epidemic, particularly among high-performing women.

Now, we pivot.

This chapter is about moving from imbalance to integration – it's about how we rebuild. It is a call to reclaim *holistic success* –

where your ambition, wellness, and relationships do not compete, but cooperate. It is about redefining success so that you thrive at work and flourish at home. Because the boardroom is not the pinnacle of your life – it is just one room in the house of your greatness.

Let's begin by dismantling some of the most damaging myths that keep us stuck in imbalance.

THE MYTH OF PERFECT BALANCE

One of the most dangerous ideas women are taught about balance is that it requires giving equal time to everything, every single day. This myth is not only impractical, it's emotionally exhausting. It sets us up to feel like failures before the day even begins.

Real balance is not about symmetry – it's about *synergy*. It's not about perfectly dividing time between work, home, and self. It's about designing a life where each of those parts *supports* the others. Some days your work will take the lead. Other days, your health or your family will need more of you. And that is okay.

The secret is intentional presence. When you're at work, be there fully. When you're with your family, connect wholeheartedly. When you rest, release the guilt. It is not how you divide your hours, but how you *honour your energy* that creates true balance.

This kind of balance begins not on your calendar – but in your *consciousness*. It begins with a clear alignment between your values and how you spend your time.

THE WEEKLY BALANCE PLANNER: A TOOL FOR INTENTIONAL LIVING

Every Sunday evening, I pause and ask myself four questions:

- Does my upcoming schedule reflect what matters most to me?
- Is there space for rest, renewal, and relationship?
- Have I protected time for those I love?
- Am I chasing success, or creating significance?

If I'm misaligned, I make changes. I don't wait for a crisis to reset; I correct course early. These small adjustments accumulate into a well-balanced life.

Balance is not found – it is *created*. And powerful women create it on purpose.

THE SILENT CRISIS OF HIGH-PERFORMING WOMEN

Behind every powerful woman who *"has it all together"* on paper, there may be a soul running on empty. We are celebrated in the workplace while slowly losing connection at home. We're achieving milestones at the expense of our health. Our calendars are full, but our hearts are empty.

This is not the success we want.

Now we move from awareness to *empowerment* – from identifying the problem to implementing solutions.

CONTENTMENT: THE FOUNDATION OF INNER BALANCE

Striving for excellence in life and leadership is admirable, but it must be grounded in contentment. Contentment is not the opposite of ambition; it's the foundation of inner balance. It means being at peace with where you are while still pressing towards your goals.

Words like fulfilled, joyful, and comforted reflect emotional states that fuel resilience and well-being. While they may seem attainable only in perfect conditions, true contentment is rooted in perspective, not circumstances.

When life feels uncertain or disappointing, it's normal to feel anxious or disillusioned – but you don't have to remain there. You can choose to shift your emotional state. If you're struggling right now, these four keys can guide you towards contentment, despite what you may be facing.

1. Choose to Be Content

The first key to contentment is to realise that it is not a feeling that descends on you once life is perfect. It is a deliberate decision – a mindset you adopt regardless of the chaos around you. It's the quiet inner knowing that while things may not be where you want them to be, you are still safe, still progressing, still enough.

Choosing contentment doesn't mean ignoring your struggles; it means learning to hold peace in one hand while carrying your purpose in the other. It is the decision to say, *"This moment may be messy, but it is meaningful."* When you practise this kind of presence, you begin to see opportunities and growth even in uncomfortable seasons.

2. Take Ownership

The second key is taking full ownership of your situation and refraining from shifting blame onto other people or external circumstances. Owning your life is a radical act of leadership. It means acknowledging that while you may not control every storm, you are responsible for how you sail through it.

There's a difference between blame and ownership. *Blame* focuses on the *past*; *ownership* empowers the *future*. When you take ownership of your mindset, your choices, and your healing, you reclaim the steering wheel of your life.

William Ernest Henley's immortal words, *"I am the master of my fate: the captain of my soul,"* have anchored generations through adversity. These words are often described as one of the boldest declarations of defiance and self-determination in the face of adversity. Nelson Mandela recited them behind prison bars to remind himself of the freedom that still lived within. Their message is timeless: power is not in your position – it's in your posture.

You may not have chosen the current chapter of your life, but you get to choose how the next one is written.

3. Let Go of Regret

Regret is one of the heaviest emotions to carry. It locks us in the past and chains us to what could have been. But here's the truth: your past does not have the power to disqualify your future unless you permit it.

Letting go of regret doesn't mean pretending mistakes didn't happen. It means learning from them, forgiving yourself, and deciding to move forward. Every person who has ever achieved anything of significance has a chapter they don't read out loud. What matters is not what happened – what matters is what you choose to do now.

When you release regret, you create space for healing. You quiet the inner critic and awaken the inner champion. You stop obsessing over missed exits and start looking forward to new destinations. And in doing so, you restore your emotional energy – energy that can now fuel your goals instead of your guilt.

4. Be True to Yourself

Authenticity isn't just a buzzword – it's your compass. The more aligned you are with your values, your purpose, and your truth, the more grounded and balanced you become.

Being true to yourself starts with radical honesty. What do you truly want, not what others expect? What lights you up? What drains you? What dreams have you buried?

When you stop living someone else's version of success, you unlock a deeper fulfilment – the kind that fuels ambition without burning you out. This doesn't mean your life will mirror anyone else's. It means it will finally reflect you. And that is the most powerful story you could ever write.

As a woman on the path to the boardroom, know this: you're allowed to chase excellence without losing your peace. You can dream big and rest deeply. You can want more and still be enough.

True success is harmony – between who you are, what you do, and how you live.

COUNTERACTING THE NOISE: PROTECTING YOUR MENTAL SPACE

- *The power of words on mental well-being*

I've said this before: words are powerful. They either nourish your vision or drain your vitality. Protecting your mental space isn't a luxury – it's a leadership practice.

Two people can share the same environment, but their outlooks differ based on the words they consistently consume. Positive words uplift; negative ones drain. In this digital age, outrage-driven content is designed to hijack your attention and stir fear. It's called *rage bait*, and it works by triggering emotional responses. But you don't have to take the bait.

Guard your subconscious. Choose stories that inspire and edify, not those that breed anxiety. Curate your content like your wardrobe – unfollow what doesn't serve you. Mute noise that clouds your self-worth.

Use technology with boundaries. Begin and end your day without scrolling. Set screen-time limits. Create mental oases – through meditation, affirmations, or stillness – that restore clarity.

Your input shapes your outlook. Feed your mind words that affirm your worth and ignite your growth. You are the gatekeeper of your mental space. Protect it fiercely. Lead from it wisely.

RECLAIMING CONTROL: WHEN WORK DEMANDS TOO MUCH

In Chapter 8, we discussed how overly demanding employers, unchecked ambition, and poor execution habits prevent many women from disconnecting from work. In this section, let's explore practical strategies to reclaim control.

One of the surest ways of getting promoted is investing all your efforts towards helping your employer reach their goals. This often starts with your immediate supervisor or team lead. Throughout my professional career, I have always placed a high premium on being loyal to the leaders that I serve. As a result, my various employers were able to make some groundbreaking achievements during my employment. A notable example was my co-founding role of the Financial Intelligence Centre (FIC) at the Bank of Namibia in 2007. My loyalty was acknowledged and rewarded – I was firstly promoted to the position of Deputy Director of Financial Investigations and Analysis with the FIC, and later to Director of Finance and Administration at the young age of 34 years.

That said, I'm fully aware that loyalty is not always reciprocated or rewarded. Leadership sometimes falls into the hands of flawed people, and loyalty gets abused through excessive work demands.

As an employee who aims to break into the boardroom, your strong loyalty and willingness to go the extra mile can accelerate your rise – just be careful it isn't taken advantage of. Ambitious and eager to please, you may not immediately recognise when your employer's demands have become excessive – here are some red flags to help you spot when that line has been crossed.

RED FLAGS THAT YOUR LOYALTY IS BEING EXPLOITED

The first red flag is a decline in your emotional and mental well-being. Granted, other factors outside work can lead to this decline. However, suppose you are genuinely feeling overworked, and objective factors such as your workload and work hours support that feeling. In that case, the chances are that the demands of your employer have become excessive.

The second red flag is an abnormal preoccupation with work activities to the point that you do not have time to invest in other aspects of your personal life. We all have 24 hours in a day, which must be distributed proportionally to work, enhancing our personal lives, and sleep. If you constantly find insufficient time for the last two, there's likely a problem. Here are some steps you can take to address the situation:

1. Initiate a Clarity Conversation

When work feels overwhelming, the first step towards reclaiming control is seeking clarity, not through confrontation, but through courageous communication. Often, excessive demands are not a sign of personal failure, but the result of misaligned expectations between you and your team leader.

Schedule a one-on-one conversation and approach it as a *strategic alignment* session, not a complaint. Come prepared to lead the discussion with intention:

- Present your current responsibilities and workload.
- Ask which tasks are most critical in the short term.
- Propose timelines that reflect both urgency and sustainability.

Framing the conversation around productivity, not pressure, creates a tone of collaboration. It signals that you are not just reacting – you are thinking ahead, managing proactively, and leading yourself well.

Most leaders don't expect perfection, but they value clarity, initiative, and ownership. And when you advocate for alignment, you model the maturity and foresight of someone destined for higher leadership. This isn't about saying "no." It's about saying "yes" to excellence, with your well-being still intact.

2. Establish Personal Boundaries

One of the most vital forms of self-leadership is the ability to draw healthy boundaries, not as a sign of resistance, but as a bold act of self-preservation. Boundaries are not walls; they are bridges that protect your energy, restore your clarity, and sustain your ability to lead with impact over time.

In high-performance environments such as the workplace, the unspoken expectation to always be available can feel relentless. But let's be clear: *availability is not the same as value.* Your highest contribution comes from your focused presence, not from your constant presence.

Communicate your boundaries with clarity and confidence. You could respond.

> *"I'll give this my full attention first thing tomorrow. Evenings are dedicated to my family."*

And remember – boundaries are not just declared; they are demonstrated. Don't reward every after-hours message with an immediate reply. Instead, model a rhythm that honours your time and trains others to do the same.

If your boundary is tested, remain calm and consistent. You could respond:

> *"I understand this feels urgent. Let's schedule a time during working hours to address it fully."*

You are not being difficult – you are being deliberate. Boundaries are not a luxury for leaders; they are a necessity. They guard your well-being, protect your priorities, and ensure that you lead not from depletion, but from a place of strength. Choosing to protect your space is not selfish. It's strategic. It's the discipline of a woman who understands her value and leads accordingly.

3. Self-Advocate Effectively

One of the most powerful tools on your journey to the boardroom is your ability to advocate for yourself, not with defensiveness, but with calm, unwavering conviction. Self-advocacy isn't confrontation. It's communication. It's about making your needs known, honouring your boundaries, and ensuring your voice, value, and vision are acknowledged and respected.

To advocate well, start by owning your worth. Reflect on your impact – your growth, your contributions, your victories. Confidence isn't born from applause; it's built on clarity. When you are rooted in purpose and grounded in values, you speak with assurance, not apology.

In my coaching practice, I teach a tool called the **C.A.L.M. Framework** – because true advocacy is not a reaction, but a conscious choice.

- **C – Clarity:** Be clear about what you need and why it matters – for you, for the team, and the organisation.

- **A – Assertiveness:** Speak with calm confidence. Assertiveness isn't aggression – it's self-respect in action.

- **L – Listening:** Make room for dialogue. Advocacy isn't a monologue; it's an exchange built on mutual respect.

- **M – Meaning:** Anchor your request in a deeper purpose. Link it to outcomes that matter – performance, progress, or team cohesion.

Self-advocacy is not a skill reserved for crises. Practise it in everyday moments: in meetings when your ideas need air, in emails where your workload needs rebalancing, or in conversations where your boundaries need reinforcing. Every time you speak up, you affirm your value. Every time you name your needs, you reinforce your dignity. And every time you advocate for yourself, you lead by example, permitting other women to do the same. Above all, lead yourself first. If you don't honour your own time, voice, and well-being, it becomes difficult for others to do so. You are not merely climbing a ladder – you are reshaping what leadership looks and feels like. Let your self-advocacy reflect self-trust, not self-defence. Let it be steady, gracious, and intentional.

4. Track Your Workload and Well-Being

Sustainable leadership begins with self-awareness. Tracking your weekly workload, emotional state, and physical health reveals patterns that pressure often hides. Log your hours, note which tasks energise or drain you, and reflect on how your work impacts your sleep, mood, and relationships.

This isn't about complaining – it's about clarity. Documented patterns give you the confidence to speak up and course-correct before burnout sets in.

Pay attention to subtle warning signs such as fatigue, anxiety, and missed personal commitments – they are signals, not inconveniences.

Tracking isn't just a time management tool – it's a leadership strategy. You can't lead others well if you're ignoring your limits. Strong leaders don't just keep going – they pause, reflect, and realign.

5. Evaluate the Long-Term Fit

If your workplace continues to compromise your well-being despite your efforts, consider whether it is still aligned with your vision. You are allowed to choose environments where your gifts are honoured and your peace is preserved.

You do not owe your health to any job. Your loyalty must never cost you your sanity. Sometimes, the most empowered move is an intentional exit, not as an escape, but as a strategic decision to place yourself in an environment where your brilliance can thrive without constant burnout.

TURNING AMBITION INTO A SUSTAINABLE ADVANTAGE

Without ambition, this book would not exist. It was my desire to create something meaningful – a guide for women who dare to step into the boardroom – that ignited every word on these pages. This book was birthed by ambition, and it is written for the ambitious.

Let me be clear: ambition is not the problem. It is the spark behind every innovation, every movement, every breakthrough. Ambition drives us to rise, to lead, to leave something better behind. But ambition without balance becomes a burden. When the price of progress is your peace, your health, or your relationships, it's no longer advancement – it's depletion.

True success cannot be defined by career milestones alone. It is holistic. It rests on three interconnected pillars:

1. **Professional life** – your work, your calling, your contribution to the marketplace.
2. **Personal well-being** – your mind, body, emotions, and spiritual health.
3. **Family life** – the relationships that ground you, and the people that love you, and walk with you beyond the spotlight.

These areas don't need equal hours – they need intentional energy. You may spend your day leading a team, but you can still make space in the evening for a shared meal or a moment of connection with your family. You don't need to be everywhere, all the time – you just need to be fully present where it matters most.

Balance is not a fixed formula. It is a fluid rhythm guided by purpose. And your *why* is what keeps that rhythm in motion.

If you find yourself over-invested in career goals while undernourishing your soul or your relationships, it's time to pause – not to shrink your ambition, but to realign it.

Ask yourself:

- Why do I want to succeed?
- Who am I becoming in the process?
- Will the people I love recognise me when I get there?

Ambition is a gift. But it must be stewarded wisely. You don't have to choose between impact and intimacy, achievement and inner peace. When your ambition is anchored in a deeper purpose, it becomes a sustainable advantage, not just a drive to get ahead, but a path to live and lead well.

Let your success be expansive, not expensive.

If you've been dedicating all your energy to breaking into the boardroom at the expense of your well-being and family life, let's look at some practical steps to help you reconnect with your why and realign your ambition with what matters most.

- *Own Your Past, Attitude, and Actions*

One of the most liberating steps towards sustainable success is taking full ownership – not just of your future, but of your *past* and the mindset that shaped it. Real transformation begins when you understand the deeper motivations behind your previous choices and choose healthier ways to meet those same needs moving forward.

Perhaps you've poured yourself into your career at the expense of your well-being and your home life. There may have been valid reasons. Maybe, like me, you come from humble beginnings, and you made a silent vow never to return to the struggle you witnessed growing up. Maybe your self-worth was chipped away by past experiences, and you believed that climbing the corporate ladder would finally validate your value. Or maybe, when life felt out of control in other areas, your job became your safe space – your escape, your refuge.

Whatever your story, know this: your reasons were human. They made sense in that season. But here's the truth – those needs are still asking to be met. The difference now is that you have the wisdom and power to meet them in ways that are *balanced, sustainable, and life-giving*.

Taking ownership doesn't mean carrying shame – it means choosing to lead yourself with compassion and responsibility. You get to rewrite the narrative. You get to say, *"I understand what shaped me – but it no longer defines me."*

This is where holistic success begins – not in perfection, but in self-awareness. Not in regret, but in responsibility. When you own your past, your perspective shifts. And from that place of clarity, you can build a future that honours both your ambition and your wholeness.

- *Shift Your Mindset*

Your drive to succeed likely came from a place of truth – perhaps from a deep desire to change your circumstances, prove your worth, or create a better life. Those reasons are valid. But sometimes, even valid reasons can lead us down unsustainable paths when we don't pause to examine the mindset behind them.

If you've been working yourself to the bone, sacrificing your health or your relationships to escape a past marked by scarcity or hardship, know this: you are not alone. But escaping poverty isn't just about working harder. It's also about transforming your *relationship with money*, adopting healthier financial habits, and dismantling the scarcity mindset that says, *"I must keep proving, earning, and striving to feel secure."*

Likewise, your self-worth cannot be anchored to titles, promotions, or the size of your salary. Those things are *outcomes* – not your identity. True self-worth is rooted in knowing who you are, not what you've achieved. It's about recognising your intrinsic value as a human being, worthy of rest, joy, and love, regardless of your job title.

When you pursue the boardroom from a place of passion and purpose, not pressure and performance, you shift from chasing success to *living* it. You stop running from your past and begin walking towards your future with clarity and intention.

Because here's the truth: no job, no matter how prestigious, can heal unresolved wounds. At some point, your career will pause through retirement, illness, transition, or change. And when that happens, the parts of yourself you neglected will still be waiting for you.

Don't use ambition as a distraction. Face what needs healing. Address what's unfinished. And from that place of wholeness, pursue the boardroom with confidence – not as a way to prove your worth, but as an expression of it.

- *Consider Alternatives*

Now that you have resolved to succeed holistically, consider the practical steps that you can take to make this desire a reality.

If you have the privilege of working from home, try incorporating personal moments into your workday. This is called work–life integration. For example, this could be picking up the kids from school, helping them with their homework, or enjoying quality time with your spouse or partner, then making up those work hours later in the day. If your current role or organisational culture does not support your desire for balance, you might need to step back and look for an organisation or role that supports your newfound ambition while still providing a path to the boardroom. Though this may feel like a radical step, it might be what you need to ensure that you are both a public and private success.

MASTERING EXECUTION FOR GREATER IMPACT

If you struggle to complete tasks quickly and efficiently, understanding why is the first step towards improving your productivity and freeing you to disconnect from work when necessary, to focus on the important areas of your life. Once you identify the cause, finding the solution becomes so much easier.

Inefficiency in execution doesn't just waste time – it drains your energy, clouds your confidence, and disrupts your ability to lead with clarity. As a woman rising into leadership, mastering execution is essential. It's not about doing more, but doing what matters most — with focus and purpose.

Start by identifying where your time is slipping away. Is it poor planning? Task switching? Delayed decisions? Once you know, address it with intention.

Begin each week with a focused planning session. Set your priorities and block time for deep, uninterrupted work. Let your calendar reflect what's truly important, not just what's urgent. Use tools such as digital planners or structured journals to track tasks and deadlines, and batch similar work to maintain momentum.

Introduce a daily shutdown ritual – a few quiet minutes to review what was done, what will carry forward, and to mentally release the workday. This clears your head and allows you to fully rest.

Finally, protect your time by saying *NO* to tasks that don't align with your goals. Delegate where possible, automate where practical, and always lead with intention.

Efficient execution is a leadership skill – one that creates room for clarity, strategy, and sustained balance.

STRENGTHENING DOMESTIC SUPPORT: PARTNERSHIPS, NOT SACRIFICE

True boardroom success must be underpinned by a solid foundation at home. You cannot build a thriving professional life on the crumbling ground of exhaustion, resentment, or isolation. And yet, this is the unspoken reality for many women, carrying the full weight of both career and domestic life in silence. But let me be clear: *domestic support is not a luxury; it's a leadership imperative.*

If you have a partner, it's time to shift from *silent frustration* to *intentional partnership*. Open the conversation with clarity:

- Are our domestic roles equitable?
- What responsibilities can we reassign?
- How can we structure our home life to support my professional growth, not sabotage it?

These are not petty questions – they are foundational negotiations. Your career deserves the same support structures often assumed for male professionals. A partner who cannot or will not hold space for your calling will, eventually, stifle it.

Whether you're navigating leadership with or without a partner – by choice or circumstance – understand this: **asking for help is not a weakness; it is wisdom**. Consider practical support systems:

- Hire help if financially possible.
- Enlist extended family, trusted friends, or community networks.
- Explore co-parenting plans, carpooling, shared school runs, or grocery delivery services.

Stop trying to earn your worth through exhaustion. The goal is not to do it all. The goal is to ensure it all gets done well, with your wellness intact.

And to the women who don't have children or partners: society may not say it out loud, but your time is just as sacred. Use your autonomy to build rhythms that protect your energy, fuel your passions, and make space for rest and restoration.

Whether single or partnered, mother or not, your right to thrive is non-negotiable. Domestic support is not a side conversation – it is a strategic pillar in your leadership journey. You're not just leading at work; you're building a life. Make sure it sustains you, not one that silently erodes you.

SUMMARY: OWN YOUR WHOLENESS

True success isn't just about boardroom titles, accolades, or high-level influence – it's about living a life where your ambition, well-being, and relationships are in harmony. As a woman leader, you are not required to choose between career excellence and personal fulfilment. You are powerful enough to build both. It begins with intentionality: owning your story, aligning with your purpose, and creating support systems that sustain your vision. Let your success be the kind that doesn't leave parts of you behind. Because the boardroom is not your final destination – it's simply one room in the house of your greatness.

CHAPTER 10
THE POWER OF PERSONAL BRANDING

"Products are built in factories, but a brand is built in the hearts and minds of people."

Just like there are different brands of similar products, you also have your unique brand that separates you from other people, and it is the quality of this personal brand that will get you into the boardroom. This dispels a common myth that branding is only for businesses. In reality, each one of us has a brand, regardless of whether we intentionally cultivate it or not – and I will explain why as we progress through this chapter.

The other day, while at a convenience store to buy some apple juice, I was faced with a choice between two brands. In my opinion, apple juice is just apple juice; it all tastes the same. What complicated the matter in this instance was the 12 Namibian dollar price difference between the brands.

What gave Brand A the audacity to ask for so much more? That was the question that was making cartwheels in my mind. Suddenly, I felt as if I would be missing out on something if I went with Brand B. Something must be lacking for it to be priced so low. Granted, Brand A is the more popular choice when it comes to fruit juices, but not N$12 more in my opinion.

Brand B was not a total unknown – it is a strong competitor in the market. Without revealing my ultimate choice, which I will let you guess after considering my accounting background, this experience got me thinking about the power of branding in influencing our choices. Brand power is the intangible difference that makes one product stand out as different when there is no difference. In my situation, the apple juice was the product, but the brand was the name on each bottle and its perceived promise to the market.

This is what makes the subject of branding so fascinating – the value its target market ascribes to it is determined in the hearts and minds of its consumers. It is not about the actual or monetary value of a product, but its perceived value, in other words, how much its consumers are willing to pay for it.

They say matters of the heart are complex, and it is true when it comes to branding. I have seen people make purchases that are mind-bogglingly illogical to me, yet they're worthwhile to them. Take the wildly popular Stanley Flowstate Tumbler, for example. I honestly do not know why anyone would pay N$1300 for an insulated drink container, but people do. Not only that, but they also seem to feel good about themselves while carrying it. So clearly, it's not just about the functionality of the Tumbler – it's about how it makes its owners *feel*.

That's the power of branding. People are willing to pay a premium for a brand name if it makes them feel a particular way. We might not understand this law, but it works. And by understanding its principles and application, we can apply it not only to build powerful products and service-based brands, but also to create boardroom-breaking personal brands.

Feelings matter – because they influence hearts and minds, attracting or repelling loyalty. World-renowned poet and civil rights activist Maya Angelou said some powerful words concerning this subject: "I've learned that people will forget what you said, people will forget what you did, but they will never forget how you made them feel." Wow, this is profound. Again, we see it's not about quantifiable and identifiable acts or omissions; it's about the subjective emotions that are evoked as a result of those actions. So, if you want to build a compelling brand, you cannot rely solely on logic – you must also appeal to emotion.

As we conclude this book, I want us to take a deeper dive into how you can develop a powerful personal brand and leverage it to occupy your seat in the boardroom. Every promotion involves several key stakeholders, and you need to know who they are because they are the ones who have to buy into your brand as being boardroom-ready. If you were a product or service, we would call them your target market. That's not to say that everyone else doesn't matter – your brand has to be consistent across the entire organisation – but these key promotion stakeholders are the ultimate decision makers.

For our purposes, let's define your brand as your reputation amongst your key promotion stakeholders – essentially, their opinion of you.

UNDERSTANDING PERSONAL BRAND DYNAMICS

- *What Is Your Brand?*

What shapes the opinion your key promotion stakeholders have of you? Their perception of your character, skills, and values is based on their experiences with you. According to the *Harvard Business Review*, these experiences are formed with every interaction that you have with these stakeholders. Does this mean their opinion of you can change based on how they experience each interaction with you? Absolutely. Now you may say, "Wait a minute, Estelle. That's not fair. How can I control how other people judge or perceive who I am or what I can do based on their subjective interpretations of their interactions with me?" As harsh as it may seem, unfortunately, people judge you based on how you present yourself – it's a reality of the professional world. The most successful investor of our generation, billionaire Warren Buffett, famously said, "It takes 20 years to build a reputation and five minutes to ruin it. If you think about that, you'll do things differently."

Although Buffett's words acknowledge how fragile and sensitive a personal brand can be, the Oracle of Omaha also tells us that our actions are the key to maintaining a strong brand. That is why he mentions doing things differently.

Contrary to another common myth, a brand's power is not just in its appearance but also in its actions, culture, and values. This means the power of your brand is in your hands. How you show up is what will ultimately determine its worth. That is empowering.

- *Your Reputation is Your Stock Price*

To help you consistently act in ways that build and strengthen your brand, think of yourself as a company listed on a major stock exchange. In this analogy, you are listed on the stock market of life, and your brand is the sentiment surrounding the value of your stock. When people see the promise of future returns – because you consistently deliver and perform well – they invest in you. On the flip side, they bypass you and avoid investing in you when they do not see any promise of future returns due to a constant failure to meet expectations.

As you work on building a powerful brand, take stock of where you are right now. What is the current sentiment around your stock value? Are you attracting or repelling investment? What promise is your brand communicating to your key promotion stakeholders? Is it of future returns or potential losses? Granted, no one can definitively predict what tomorrow holds, but you *can* build your brand in such a way that reassures people of your continued high performance.

Just as the wrong actions can ruin your reputation, the right actions can repair it. That is why share prices on the stock market fluctuate. When an underperforming company starts communicating the potential for improved prospects by investing in its future through new acquisitions, technologies, products, or talent, its share price normally increases. This is because investor sentiment around the future performance of the company becomes more positive, driving up demand for its shares.

The inverse is also true. When a high-performing company misses its targets, lags behind its competition in terms of innovation, or becomes embroiled in a scandal, its share price usually decreases. This is triggered by investors selling off their shares due to reduced confidence in their ability to generate future returns. The only way the company can redeem its share price is by correcting its actions to align with investor expectations.

In both cases, the message is the same: brand building is a fluid and continuous process. This busts the third brand myth – the idea that once your brand has been established, you don't have to work on it anymore. In reality, a brand's impact is dependent on constant refinement. That's good news because even if the sentiment around your brand is low right now, you can still improve it.

The key lies in shifting others' perception of you. The first step is adjusting your attitude and actions to show that you are knowledgeable, trustworthy, reliable, and a pleasure to work with.

People respond to what you wear – in terms of both the clothes that you put on, but also the character traits that you present. If you wear confidence, you'll be known as a confident person. Wear reliability, and you'll be viewed as a reliable person. The traits you choose to "wear" become the foundation of your personal brand. Keep backing them up through your attitude and actions. In no time, you will see your share price soar as positive sentiment around your future value increases.

HOW TO DISCOVER YOUR BRAND DNA

What happens when you enter a new space and you have to build your brand from scratch? This was my situation when I started E-merge Coaching in February 2021.

Before the launch of the business, most of the people I shared my plans with would ask the same question: What's going to be different about your practice? Personal development coaches were a dime a dozen, so what would set mine apart?

Although some of the conversations felt more like interrogations than genuine curiosity, I did not get offended by the question. Instead, I saw those questions as an opportunity to create the E-merge Coaching brand and gain clarity within myself as to what it was.

As I reflected, I realised that the answer was layered and comprised of four basic questions:

How was I going to stand out?

How was I going to make an impact?

How was I going to look different from my competitors?

How was I going to distinguish myself from them?

To answer these questions effectively, I had to draw from my *why* – my purpose and reason for wanting to be a coach. That purpose would become the seed from which E-merge Coaching would be conceived, giving it its unique DNA.

This DNA would enable me to stand out as a coach and make an impact. It would also give me a unique appearance and voice to set me apart from my competitors. After some self-reflection, I defined my purpose as helping people and organisations become better versions of themselves.

It was this purpose that gave me the name E-merge, which reflected it perfectly. To *emerge* is to rise or come out from a concealed place – and that's exactly what I aimed to do: help my clients unleash their hidden greatness. The name carries a direct message to anyone who engages with my brand – it's an invitation to step out and show the world the fullness of their potential.

To have a significant impact, my brand had to reflect my passion and compassion. To shape it with intention, I had to ask myself three questions. The first was: *What am I passionate about?* The answer was clear – I'm passionate about helping people and businesses succeed.

The second was: *Who do I have compassion for?* This involved identifying who I wanted to serve and the problems that I wanted to help them solve. I drew from my personal experiences and marketplace journeys as a career professional and entrepreneur to answer this question.

In March 2018, I managed to complete the Two Oceans half marathon in Cape Town after a lifetime of struggling to run for any prolonged period. That experience gave me a deep appreciation of how to overcome personal barriers and developed a desire to help others who wanted to achieve personal transformation in their lives.

My ability to break into the boardroom early on in my professional career and my success as an entrepreneur in the health food industry developed my compassion for young professionals and small to medium business owners striving to grow. I was going to help young professionals climb the corporate ladder to become C-suite executives and help small- to medium-sized enterprise owners grow and transform their businesses. These answers gave birth to my title and professional brand as an Executive, Business, and Transformational Coach, Author, and Speaker.

The third question I asked myself was: *What natural gifts, talents, and skills do I possess that can assist me in pursuing my passion and compassion?* I believe our natural gifts and talents are our Creator's way of telling us our brand's unique offering to the world. So, do you know what your natural gifts and talents are? Or do you feel that you don't have any? Maybe you believe you have them, but you are struggling to identify them.

If you fall in either of the last two categories, I want to start by reassuring you that you do have unique gifts and talents. We all do. It's what I call your "bent". These innate gifts, whether one or many, are sufficient for you to make a significant impact in this life.

The reason many people think they do not have talents is because they fail to see how they can leverage their talents to make an impact. This belief is reinforced by a society that encourages us to focus on in-demand occupations, as opposed to those that align with our innate abilities. There is wisdom in aligning with career trends, but I believe a better approach would be to integrate your natural inclinations with these trends, rather than neglecting them in favour of what's popular.

So, how do you discover your gifts and talents? You take note of the things that you love doing and are effortlessly good at. Activities or concepts that get you excited and draw you in without much burden. Secondly, you take note of the abilities that other people often compliment you on. In fact, some people may even tell you directly that those are your natural gifts and talents.

Take a few minutes to reflect upon what these abilities could be and write them down. It does not matter how insignificant you think the ability is; note it down anyway. It could be that you are naturally funny and you make people laugh. Maybe you love telling stories, and you captivate the imagination of those around you whenever you speak. Perhaps you are a good negotiator or problem solver. Maybe your charisma allows you to mobilise people around certain causes with ease.

Your gifts could be anything – from speaking to writing, singing, cooking, organising, health and fitness, homemaking, poetry, art, sport, content creation, inspiring and motivating others, and offering guidance, just to mention a few. Whatever it is, write it down. You can even ask your confidants what they think your gifts and talents are.

Now that you have completed this exercise, you should have a clearer understanding of your innate abilities. They are the foundation of your brand. Even if some of them may not directly align with the technical skills needed to break into the boardroom, they are a part of who you are, and you can use them to create rapport with your key promotion stakeholders.

It is also important to note that you may not be flawlessly proficient in applying your gifts and talents, but that does not mean they are non-existent. They have to be nurtured and developed over time, through continuous practice and the acquisition of new skills to enhance ability.

As I pointed out earlier, even though I believed I had the natural gifts and talents to run a successful coaching practice, I still had to obtain the necessary qualifications to help me apply them. In November 2024, I obtained an MBA with a specialisation in Coaching, Mentoring, and Leadership from York St John University in the UK. I also obtained some key coaching certifications, including an Executive and Management Coaching certification from the University of Cape Town, as well as certifications as a Life Coach and Life Purpose Coach (UK). I combined the skills I obtained with these qualifications with the technical skills I developed as a corporate executive and an entrepreneur to create my unique brand offering.

A convergence of my passion and compassion, together with my gifts, talents, and skills, allowed me to operate in my sweet spot. Here, my efforts are maximised for impact as I pursue my purpose. This means I am never bored when I am engaged in E-merge's business. It never feels like work; rather, it feels like the fulfilment of a calling. I am not just giving you some nice theoretical knowledge; my brand's results have spoken for themselves.

By the end of 2024, E-merge Coaching had impacted thousands of individuals and collaborated with a wide range of corporate institutions across both the public and private sectors throughout various regions of the country. Through powerful speaking engagements, group coaching, and one-on-one sessions, the message of transformation and empowerment continued to spread. My debut book, *Breaking Barriers*, gained significant traction both locally and internationally, reaching readers across Africa, Europe, North America, and the Middle East. A proud milestone was achieved when the book was featured on a billboard in New York's iconic Times Square. It went on to become a national bestseller by a Namibian author and ranked among the top sellers at Exclusive Books Namibia, standing alongside some of the world's most celebrated authors.

THE FOUR KEYS TO A WINNING PERSONAL BRAND

Time and again, I've been asked what my winning recipe has been in these short four years. Although there are several things that I had to be intentional about, these are the four key ones. They also serve to crystalise some of the points you have seen in my brand-building journey above. As you go through them, think about how you can apply them in your own context as you endeavour to build your own unique boardroom-breaking brand.

1. Identify Your Unique Value Proposition

Famous management expert Gary Hamel once said, "Sameness is a recipe for mediocrity." When you look and sound like everyone else competing for the same promotion, you risk coming across as mediocre. You've probably heard many times that the world is now a global village, but this may never have impacted you directly until now. When it comes to the world of work, what we are seeing and will continue to see is increased global job competition. This means that you will be competing for the same job as people from another continent.

Even locally, more and more people are graduating from tertiary institutions with the same qualifications and looking for the same jobs at the same salary level. So, the real question you should ask yourself is: *How am I going to stand out? What can I offer my employer that the others cannot easily duplicate?* The answers you get are the unique offerings that you will package into your Value Proposition Box.

Elements of Your Value Proposition Box

- *Character*

The beauty of character is that you can forge it into whatever you desire. Regardless of background, gender, or race, we all get to choose the values and principles that we are going to live by, who we are going to be and what we are going to stand for. Embodying traits such as honesty, integrity, hard work, loyalty, faithfulness, humility, and teachability will set you apart from your competition all the time. You can choose that no one will be as loyal to the company as you or as hard-working as you.

- *Competencies*

Show up and market yourself in line with your unique competencies. These include your unique experiences, past accolades, designations, exposures, skills, qualifications, knowledge, gifts, and talents. Your Curriculum Vitae is not a piece of paper; it's a living testament of the key competencies that you add to each day. Personally, when I show up in my business engagements, I do so as a bestselling author, coach, speaker, Forensic Accountant, and non-executive director serving on public and private sector boards. I also show up as a former Director of Finance at the Bank of Namibia, former Chairperson of the Namibian Financial Institutions Supervisory Authority (NAMFISA), co-founder of the Namibian Financial Intelligence Centre, a former member of the Presidential High-Level Panel on the Namibian Economy and 2022 inductee into the Namibian Business Hall of Fame. It's not that I display any of these titles on the outside when I am on business, but I wear them on the inside, and I carry myself as someone who has held or is currently holding them. Even when in doubt, I use them to remind myself of the journey I have travelled and the battles I have conquered. It is only when responding to new opportunities that I use them as part of my profile because they are a part of my Value Proposition Box.

- *External Appearance*

Whether you like it or not, people judge you based on your appearance. This doesn't necessarily mean they're being shallow; it just means they want to deal with someone who takes themselves seriously enough to dress well, smell good, and look presentable. Remember, you might think of yourself as being highly self-disciplined, but when it comes to your brand, what matters is not what *you* think about yourself — it's how others perceive you.

Your attitude and mindset should tell your key promotion stakeholders that they have found the right woman for the job. Your look, walk, and talk should tell everyone you mean business and that you are a candidate for the boardroom. Here's a secret about promotion: it's not so much about surprise as it is about confirmation. Everyone should be able to see it coming when you get promoted.

- *Reputation*

Every time you interact with others, it is an opportunity to reinforce your brand. Be known for your professionalism and leadership. All your actions should align with the executive that you want to be. For example, you can't expect to lead in the boardroom when you are known for staying silent in meetings. Even if you have nothing meaningful to contribute (which should not be often), make your presence felt – greet people and engage in the conversation.

2. Build Networks

Robert Kiyosaki, author of one of my favourite personal finance development books, once famously said, "*The richest people in the world look for and build networks; everyone else looks for work.*" For our purposes, we can interpret this quote to mean the professionals with the biggest personal brands focus on building networks, whilst those with the smallest or non-existent brands just do the bare minimum required by their job descriptions.

Your network is a reflection of your brand's value. This is because networking is a powerful way to build your reputation. Your network represents who you know, but your reputation represents who knows *you*. The larger your network, the greater your reputation. Start building your network today, and it is as simple as speaking to one new person at every event that you attend. Networking is simply having meaningful conversations with people, and the best way to do this is by taking a genuine interest in others. Ask them about themselves, listen carefully, and respond thoughtfully. Trust me, it works every time.

In today's digital world, you can also grow your network online, especially on platforms such as LinkedIn. Engaging meaningfully with others there can boost your brand significantly, as fellow professionals can endorse you for various skills, elevating your credibility.

As you grow your network, remember that true leadership means lifting others as you climb. One of the greatest barriers women face is not always external – it's how we treat one another. Supporting other women, rather than sabotaging their success, strengthens the collective influence of women in leadership. Celebrate their wins, advocate for them in rooms they're not in, and choose collaboration over competition. When one woman breaks into the boardroom, it's a victory – but when we rise together, it becomes a movement.

3. Send a Consistent Message

When it comes to the digital world, consistency is critical in building a powerful brand. Not only do you have to do this on your platforms, but your offline actions matter too. You need to ensure that if you were ever captured on camera and those images or videos were posted online, your brand would not be ruined.

I have seen people getting dismissed from their jobs for non-related work activities that were captured online and somehow linked to their workplace. In 2021, during some civil unrest in South Africa, video footage of a young man looting from a Woolworths store and leaving the scene in a luxurious Mercedes Benz sedan went viral across the world. Dubbed the "Woolies Looter", the young man not only went on to face criminal prosecution but lost a job opportunity in the United Kingdom. His moment of misguided excitement led to life-long career implications for the young man, ruining his brand globally. Although this is an extreme example, cases with similar personal brand implications have transpired.

What you post online really matters. Maintain the same voice, tone, values, and message on all your platforms. The message is: I belong in the boardroom.

4. Strive For Excellence

Excellence is the bedrock of a strong brand. It confirms and reinforces the positive opinions your key promotion stakeholders have of you, further strengthening your brand. When you strive for excellence in every task, no matter how small, you build a reputation of reliability and high standards. It is not about perfection, but about continuous improvement. Strive to be more effective and efficient in everything you do and aim to get it right the first time around.

These four keys have unlocked the power of personal branding for me throughout my professional career and entrepreneurial journey, making more and more people choose E-merge for their personal and business coaching. I have no doubt that, if you apply them consistently, you'll see the same – if not greater – success in your own journey.

SUMMARY: YOUR BRAND IS YOUR TICKET

You are more than your qualifications or job title – *you are a brand*. The way people perceive your character, values, and ability to lead is your greatest promotional asset.

A strong personal brand speaks before you enter the room and lingers long after you've left. It commands attention, attracts trust, and drives decisions. So, build a brand that evokes confidence, delivers excellence, and inspires others.

Your boardroom seat doesn't come from chance – it's earned through the brand you build. Apply the four keys of value, network, consistency, and excellence. Let your brand work for you, and watch the doors open to the boardroom and beyond.

CONCLUSION
THE BOARDROOM IS YOURS TO CLAIM

Breaking into the Boardroom was never just about a title, a seat at the table, or climbing the corporate ladder – it was about discovering the power that already resides within you. Through every chapter, you've been equipped to lead with confidence, strategy, purpose, and heart.

We've uncovered the internal blocks, external pressures, and societal expectations that have held women back for far too long. But more importantly, we've shattered myths, challenged limiting beliefs, and unlocked the tools needed to rise – authentically and unapologetically.

Remember, the boardroom is not reserved for a select few. It belongs to those with vision, resilience, and the courage to show up fully as themselves. You don't need permission to lead – you simply need the conviction to do so.

Now, it's your turn.

- Speak up.
- Show up.
- Take up space.
- Build your brand.
- Break the glass ceiling – and bring others with you.

Let us be women who celebrate, support, collaborate, and elevate. Let us be the generation of women who not only break into the boardroom but who hold the door open for others to walk through.

ABOUT THE AUTHOR

Estelle Tjipuka is an Executive, Business, and Transformational Coach with a passion for developing leaders and driving personal and professional transformation. A sought-after speaker and thought leader, she is the bestselling author of *Breaking Barriers*, the *Breaking Barriers Workbook*, and *The 30-Day Self-Confidence Journal*. Her work continues to empower thousands of professionals, individuals, and entrepreneurs across Namibia and beyond.

A forensic accountant by profession, Estelle brings nearly three decades of leadership experience. Her dynamic background spans forensic accounting, governance, entrepreneurship, and executive leadership, allowing her to guide individuals and organisations to achieve higher levels of performance, purpose, and impact.

She is the former Director of Finance at the Bank of Namibia and former Chairperson of the Namibia Financial Institutions Supervisory Authority (NAMFISA) – Namibia's regulator for the non-bank financial sector. Estelle also co-founded Namibia's Financial Intelligence Centre (FIC), where she played a pivotal role in drafting and enacting the country's first Financial Intelligence Act (Act 3 of 2007). A Certified Fraud Examiner (CFE) and Certified Anti-Money Laundering Specialist (CAMS), she is widely respected for her expertise in financial forensics.

Estelle has served on numerous boards in both the public and private sectors and was appointed to the Presidential High-Level Panel on the Namibian Economy by the Late President, His Excellency, Dr Hage G. Geingob. Through her coaching firm, E-merge Coaching, she has helped transform countless leaders and businesses, providing tailored coaching, mentorship, and strategic support.

She holds a Bachelor's degree in Forensic Investigations from the University of South Africa and completed her articles with PricewaterhouseCoopers in Windhoek. Estelle is an alumna of the International Executive Development Programme (IEDP), delivered jointly by the Wits Business School (South Africa) and London Business School (UK). She also holds certifications in Executive and Management Coaching from the University of Cape Town, as well as Life Coaching and Life Purpose Coaching from the UK.

A firm believer in lifelong learning, Estelle recently earned a Global MBA in Coaching, Mentoring, and Leadership, passed with Merit from York St John University in the UK.

In recognition of her outstanding contribution to leadership and business in Namibia, Estelle was inducted as a Laureate into the Namibian Business Hall of Fame in 2022. She is also the recipient of the **Trailblazer Award**, presented at the 2018 Africa Women Conference.

www.ingramcontent.com/pod-product-compliance
Lightning Source LLC
Chambersburg PA
CBHW020932090426
42736CB00010B/1114